AMERICAN
SIGN LANGUAGE

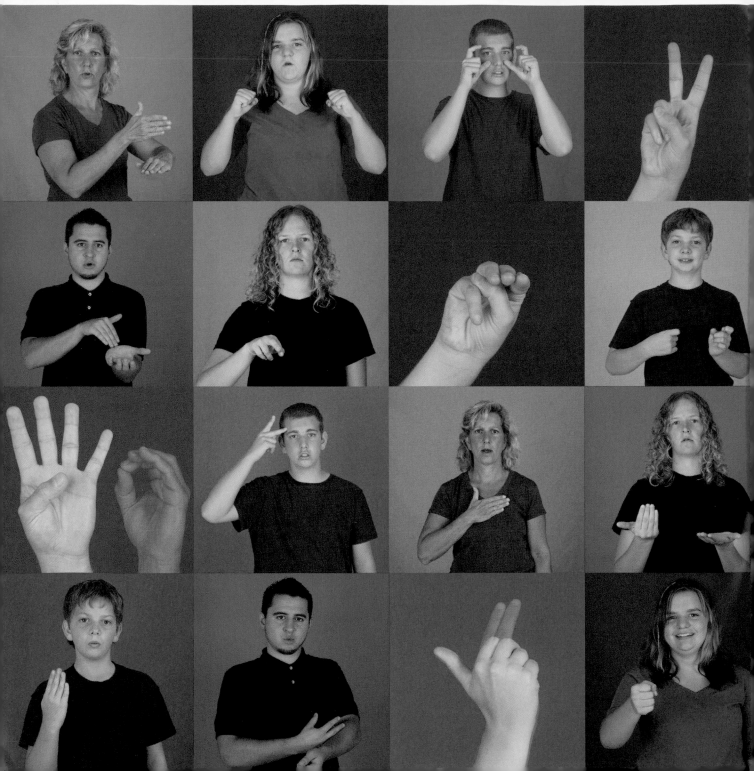

KNACK®

AMERICAN SIGN LANGUAGE

A Step-by-Step Guide to Signing

SUZIE CHAFIN

Photographs by Johnston Bell Grindstaff

KNACK®
MAKE IT EASY

Guilford, Connecticut
An imprint of The Globe Pequot Press

Editor-in-Chief: Maureen Graney
Editor: Katie Benoit
Cover Design: Paul Beatrice, Bret Kerr
Text Design: Paul Beatrice
Layout: Kevin Mak
Cover photos by Johnston Bell Grindstaff
All interior photos by Johnston Bell Grindstaff

Library of Congress Cataloging-in-Publication Data is available on
file.

ISBN 978-1-59921-514-3

Printed in the United States of America

10 9 8 7 6

Author Dedication
For my parents, John & Margie Coggins-Peckham.

Author Acknowledgments
This book would not be possible without some very important people. First, thanks to my agent, Barb Doyen, for her encouragement, help, and support. I am indebted to Maureen Graney and Katie Benoit for the opportunity to write the book and their support throughout the work. Thanks to John Grindstaff, our gifted photographer, for his artistic photographs illustrating this beautiful language. I could not have had this experience without my parents, John and Margie Coggins-Peckham. Thank you both for giving me a bilingual world. Thank you to my sister, Linda Garrelick, for not only sharing the CODA experience with me, but for her speech pathology expertise. Thanks to Nancy Jenkins, my friend and special needs specialist. Last, many thanks to my husband Andy and my four children Sam, Lauren, Jon, and James for their constant support and encouragement.

Photographer Dedication
To my family, Natalie, Jarvis, Raquel and Jake, for your endless love and support.

Photographer Acknowledgments
Thanks to the publishing team at The Globe Pequot Press, especially Maureen Graney and editor Katie Benoit for their confidence in my artistic photography to reveal the beautiful and colorful American Sign Language. Thanks to my wife, Natalie, for her countless helps being a sign master, assistant, model, and more. Thanks to my children Jarvis, Raquel, and Jake for being models and expressing in their native ASL and for their ideas in techniques. Also, thanks to my signing models, Amanda Schahn and Adrian DeHoyas for their time and help with ideas in the art of signing.

CONTENTS

INTRODUCTION

As a CODA (child of a deaf adult), I found using American Sign Language (ASL) no different than speaking English. My parents, who are both completely deaf, lived in a silent world and used their hands, eyes, and body for their ears. My mother and aunt were both born with hearing loss. My mother is profoundly deaf, and my aunt is hard of hearing and now wears a cochlear implant. My father became deaf after his mother contracted rubella, or German measles, during pregnancy. My parents, who are both smart, articulate people, met in Washington, D.C., at Gallaudet University, the world's only liberal arts university designed to meet the needs of the Deaf. Both worked for major corporations until retirement. They are living examples that hearing is not a prerequisite for success in life.

My sister and I grew up immersed in two worlds. At home we were part of the Deaf culture, attending deaf functions, deaf church services, and the very long hours of deaf social events. My childhood best friend, whose parents were both hard of hearing, was also a CODA. The hearing world waited for us at school, where we would use words and our ears to communicate and learn. Then, back at home we were part of the deaf world again.

Our family was like most families, with a few subtle differences. Instead of hollering, we used lights to grab attention. We answered the phone and doorbell like in any house but were alerted by flashing lights. We interpreted for our parents on a broad scale, including making car negotiations and doctor appointments, booking hotel reservations, calling insurance companies, holding parent-teacher conferences, ordering meals at restaurants, and so on. We argued like any parents and child, with the exception that when they had enough they could close their eyes and not "hear" us any longer. Instead of going to the movies with our parents, we went to "Deaf" clubs and watched closed captioned movies on a giant movie screen with other deaf families. As a child, I remember vividly trying to see if this "deaf thing" was all a great big joke. I would walk up behind my dad and yell as loud as I could in the hopes he would turn around. He never did.

My sister and I also learned pretty early on that the hearing world could be a tough place for the Deaf. We learned that assumptions were made about their ability to speak, drive, think, and work simply because they

couldn't hear. Mean kids said hurtful things and made fun of the Deaf community. We were inadvertently not included in variety of peer activities from Girl Scouts to soccer because our parents weren't "in the know" with the other parents. That is why I am so excited you have decided to pick up this book.

By learning ASL, the native tongue of the Deaf community, you are about to bridge a communication barrier. You'll learn a beautiful, active, vibrant language and a people rich in culture, community, and fellowship.

The Signing Basics

First, we'll begin with the signing basics—the ABCs, numbers, colors, and basic signs used in everyday conversation. In these chapters you'll learn the American Manual Alphabet, the signed equivalent of the twenty-six letters of the English alphabet. Armed with this knowledge you'll be able to finger spell words and begin conversations. You'll also learn colors, numbers (yes, even numbers are a little different than what you're used to), and basic signs to begin conversations with.

After you have the signing basics down, we'll venture into specific settings and learn phrases to use in those environments. We'll begin with small-talk phrases. These phrases are a great way to begin having conversations with the Deaf that go beyond simple finger spelling, gestures, and handwritten notes. You'll learn signs to say in social settings and be encouraged to dive into the Deaf world to learn more.

Signing for Children

Next, we'll focus on signs to teach a baby or toddler. Research proves that children who learn sign language at an early age are poised for greater success in the classroom later. The signs give babies important tools to speak to their parents before verbal words can be articulated. The signs help reduce frustration between parent and child as you learn what exactly your child is trying to communicate to you.

Perhaps you've been inspired to learn sign because you work with or are around deaf students or children with special needs. Much as with the benefits of teaching a baby to sign, many times the special needs child has words he or she wants to communicate but doesn't have the verbal ability to do so. Giving such children words with their hands allows them to speak and communicate.

Sports Signs

Coaching a team? Or maybe you're a parent on a team with a deaf child or deaf parent. Learning ASL will help you better coach and communicate with your team. In the sports chapters you'll learn key signs to use on the field and off.

Health and Safety

Are you a medical provider? Or are you a concerned family member or friend? In these chapters you'll learn not only beneficial medical signs but also protections of the Americans with Disabilities Act and tips to get more from

the doctor's visit. As a result, you'll learn how to best take care of the ones you love.

Signing in the Real World

If you have a deaf associate or employee at work, learning ASL will help you better communicate with that associate or employee. In these chapters you'll learn signs specific to employer issues. You'll also learn phrases to say around the water cooler. Creating a deaf-friendly work environment will produce a happier, more productive, and efficient place of work.

Similarly, creating a deaf-friendly worship environment will produce a more solid community. Watching a worship service in ASL is almost like watching a person dance through his or her hands. Perhaps a deaf ministry in your temple or church has inspired you to learn ASL. In these chapters you'll learn religious signs as well as gain ideas of how to have a better and more effective deaf ministry.

Through it all, you'll find that communicating with the Deaf community is not unlike communicating with the hearing world. Through ASL, you'll leap into a wonderfully intriguing and beautiful new world. So, what are you waiting for? Turn those pages and begin your journey into American Sign Language.

READY, SET, GO
Shake out those fingers and get ready to sign

So, you've decided to learn sign language. You've probably been signing your whole life—a quick wave "hello," the thumbs-up sign for good job, and, of course, the universal "OK" sign. Much like a child who goes from baby babbling to understandable words, you are about to learn the proper techniques to articulate words through your hands and body. Are you ready to begin?

The American Manual Alphabet is a great place for a beginner to start. It is the signed equivalent of the English alphabet, complete with twenty-six letters. With these letters you will be able to finger spell words when you don't know the sign. Or if you don't understand a sign, your partner can finger spell the word for you. Finger spelling is also used when somebody wants to make a point. Think of it as spelling in all caps in an e-mail—the person is drawing emphasis to a particular word or point. You will use your dominant hand

Let's Start!

- The dominant hand should be in a starting position about midchest level.

- No floppy wrists! Your wrist should be strong. Fingers should flow easily from one letter into the next.

- Face your palm away from your body to your partner.

- Try to keep the "silent" hand still. Don't cause distraction with unnecessary movement.

Proper Body Position

- Relax; you're just saying words with your hands, not performing on stage.

- Use your dominant hand. If you are right handed, this will be your right hand. If you are left handed, then use your left.

- Your primary motions will be made with the dominant hand.

- Your palm will be facing the recipient to aid word transition and understanding.

to finger spell. Simply leave the other hand at rest on your side. Don't move it around—you don't want to confuse the person you are talking to.

······· GREEN ● LIGHT ··············

Relax. Signing is not hard. Be sure to look directly at the person you are going to speak to. Don't get too close! Leave enough space for the person to see your facial expressions, body language, and signs. About 3 to 4 feet should do it. Speak or mouth the words clearly as you sign. Are you right handed or left handed? Use your dominant hand for signs that are made with one hand.

This is how *b* appears to the person you are talking to, or your reflection.

The Letter A

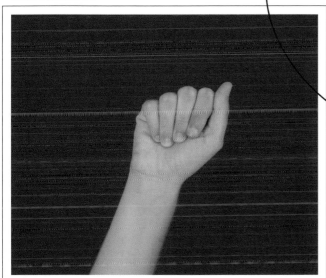

- Use your dominant hand.

- Bend your elbow so that your wrist is held in the space between your chest and face.

- Form a fist with your hand.

- Extend the thumb upward and press it tightly against the closed fingers of the fist.

The Letter B

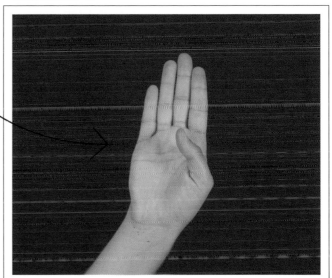

- Using your dominant hand, face your palm toward the person you are talking to.

- The four fingers—index, middle, ring, and pinky finger—will all be extended straight up.

- There is no space between the fingers.

- The thumb will be tightly closed across the middle of the palm.

1

C, D, E, & F
Relax, loosen up, and have fun with the ABCs

Forming each of the letters takes practice and time. You will find that many of the letters in the ASL alphabet actually mirror written letters, such as c, l, j and more. You will also find that many letters are similar to one another. Be careful to not accidentally substitute one letter for another. For example, *d* and *f* are often confused. Learn the letters right the first time, and you'll avoid embarrassing mistakes later.

With more than 1 million Americans being functionally deaf, ASL follows Spanish as the third-most-spoken language in the United States. ASL is taught in schools across the country as a recognized foreign language. Although the language may at first seem like awkward finger movements, you'll soon find your hands speaking a vibrant, active, and expression-filled language. Hearing people too often assume the Deaf to be disabled. As you dive into this new language you'll discover a very able community and culture.

The Letter C

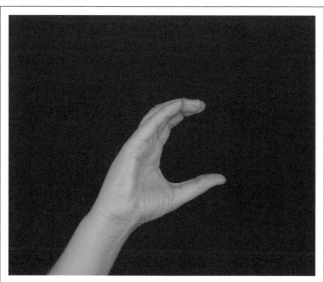

- Use your dominant hand in the space between your chest and face.

- Cup your hand to form what mimics the letter *c* in written English.

- The fingers will not have spaces between them.

The Letter D

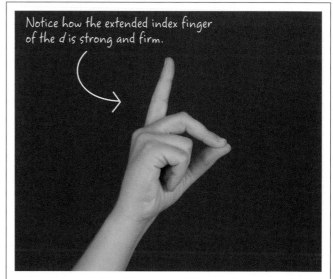

Notice how the extended index finger of the *d* is strong and firm.

- *D* uses the dominant hand.

- The index finger will be extended straight up.

- The remaining three fingers will be folded touching the thumb.

- If you are finger spelling a word, don't say each letter as you spell it but rather say the entire word.

Watch the finger placement of the thumb here. If you go too high it will look like an *s*. The thumb should sit just below the fingers.

ZOOM

Just as the English and Spanish do not share the same language, ASL is unique to the United States. More than 103 types of signed languages exist in countries all over the world. Even traveling in Great Britain you'll experience sign variances from ASL. Across countries the signs may be different, but communication can easily be achieved through gesturing, pointing, and body language.

The Letter E

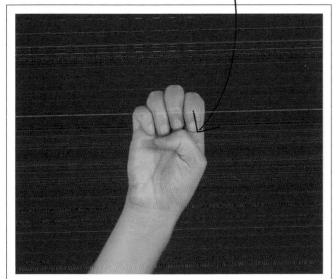

- The signs *e, s, m,* and *n* are often confused. Note where the thumb rests to see the difference.

- The thumb of the *e* is just underneath the four folded fingers of the hand.

- The back of the palm will be facing you.

- Practice signing *e, s, m,* and *n* to get used to the differences between the signs.

The Letter F

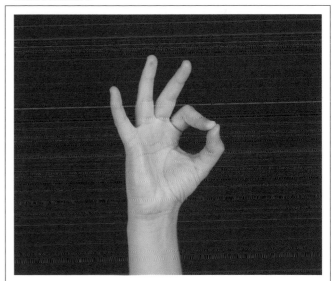

- The letter *f* is made using your dominant hand.

- The index and thumb will touch, forming an *o* like shape.

- The remaining fingers will be extended.

- There should be space between the three extended fingers.

G, H, I, & J

Soon these letters will be rolling off your fingers

Most people who meet a deaf person for the first time feel nervous and scared about trying to communicate. What if the person doesn't understand you? Are there other ways to talk to the Deaf besides sign language?

Although ASL is the backbone of communication for the Deaf, changes in technology have eroded barriers and brought the Deaf and hearing worlds closer together than ever. Need a quick response? Text messages, e-mails, and

Internet chatting enable instant communication. Most Deaf carry cell phones, using the text feature to easily and quickly communicate with family and friends. Closed captioning not only helps the Deaf "hear" television programs but also helps with literacy and provides needed information in a noisy atmosphere. Talking via telephone has never been easier through the assistance of video and telephone relay services. Aside from the physical ability to hear sound, the differences

The Letter G

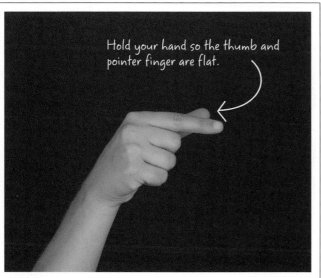

Hold your hand so the thumb and pointer finger are flat.

- Using the dominant hand, fold the middle, ring, and pinky fingers into your palm.

- Extend the thumb and index finger.

- Horizontally position the hand so the thumb and index finger are flat.

- Depending on whom you talk to or where you live, you might find a slightly different version. The alternate version uses the index finger and thumb in a vertical, not horizontal, position.

The Letter H

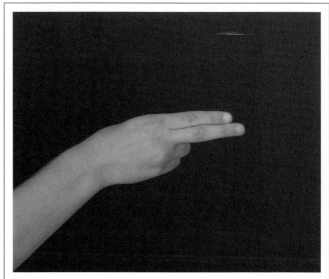

- Fold the thumb and ring and pinky finger into the palm of your hand.

- Extend the index and middle fingers.

- The fingers should be straight and rigid.

- Lay the fingers across in a horizontal position.

between the hearing and the Deaf are diminishing rapidly.

As a beginner, don't worry if you don't have all the signs for what you want to say. Use gestures, finger spell, and mouth or speak clearly what you mean. These context clues will help the person you are talking to figure out what you mean. Often he will take the time to teach you the signs you don't know.

ZOOM

All of the pictures in this book show the signs from the vantage point of the viewer, as though you are the person the picture is directed to. As you practice your signs, do them in a mirror and check to see if you match the images in the picture.

The letter j begins with a sideways i. Scoop your pinky downward until it is underneath the fist.

The Letter I

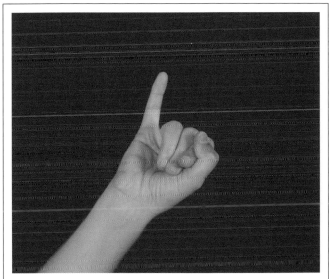

- The letter *i* is made simply by extending the pinky finger straight up.

- The remaining fingers will form a closed fist, with the thumb pressed across the fingers.

The Letter J

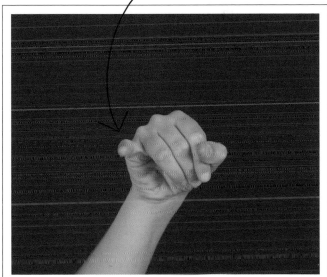

- Much like the letter *i*, begin *j* with extending the pinky finger.

- The pinky finger will be facing out to the side.

- The remaining fingers will be in a closed fist with the thumb pressed across the fingers.

- In a downward curved motion, move the pinky so it is now directly underneath the wrist.

K, L, M, & N
Don't get tired; you're halfway there

When you talk to someone it is customary to wait for pauses and breaks in the conversation before jumping in. You don't want to step all over someone else's words or cut her off before a thought is complete. The same speaking etiquette applies in ASL. Wait for your partner to have a signing pause indicating it is your turn to talk. Other visual cues let you know it is your turn to speak too: a look of question, a raised eyebrow, or a finger pointed at you.

Pepper your conversation with head nods, the verbal equivalent of a "yes," "right," or "exactly." These head nods allow your partner to know you understand what he is saying and are on the same page. If you look confused and shake your head "no," he will understand that you're lost. Don't be afraid to ask the person to repeat what he has said. Also try to use context clues to figure out what the person is saying. If you still don't understand, be sure to let the person

The Letter K

- The letter *k* is a little tricky at first. Your fingers just don't feel like they are in a natural position.

- Your thumb should be snugly placed between your middle finger and pointer fingers.

- Your middle finger will be the lowest, the thumb in the middle, and then the pointer finger almost straight up.

- Notice how the signed *k* mimics the written letter k.

The Letter L

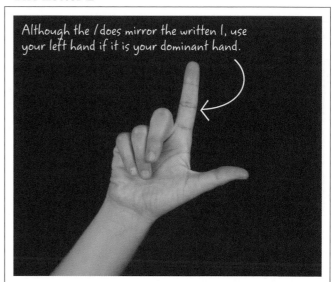

Although the *l* does mirror the written l, use your left hand if it is your dominant hand.

- Use your dominant hand to form the letter *l*.

- The index finger will extend straight up.

- The thumb will extend to the side.

- All other fingers will fold downward.

know. Don't try to continue a conversation unsure of what you should say or what was just said.

When speaking with the Deaf, also be aware that word order may not be what you are used to. For example, if you are out enjoying a burger and fries with a deaf friend, he may refer to the French fries as fries French. Being aware ahead of time of these word order differences will help you make sense and help you follow the conversation more easily.

The Letter M

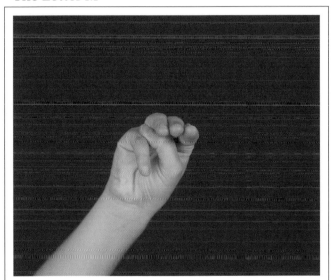

- The letter *m* can be confused with *e, s, t,* and *n*. Focus on the finger placement.

- The thumb will be underneath three folded-down fingers. Using fewer fingers indicates other letters.

- Be sure to hold the wrist still. It is hard to read a moving hand.

The Letter N

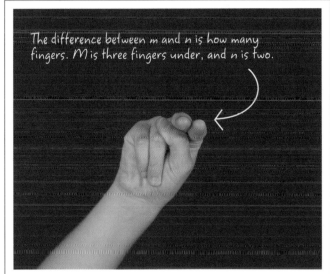

The difference between *m* and *n* is how many fingers. *M* is three fingers under, and *n* is two.

- Like *m*, *n* is easily confused. Take care with the placement of the thumb to make sure you are saying the right letter.

- The thumb will be underneath two folded-down fingers.

- If the thumb is under one more finger, it is the letter *t*; if it is over one more finger, it is the letter *m*.

O, P, Q, & R

Fingers feeling quirky? Soon you'll be a seasoned signer

Now that you're starting to get the feel of your fingers shaping letters, take a moment to really study your finger work. Are your fingers in the right position? Are your fingers relaxed or rigid? Is your arm moving with each letter? Or are you remembering to hold your arm and wrist still while forming each letter? Remembering your form will improve your readability to your partner and will keep you practicing the right way.

As you converse with a deaf person, you may notice a key word or point repeated several times. This communication technique is used to help convey emphasis. Respond back with a head nod and facial expression indicating you understand.

The Letter O

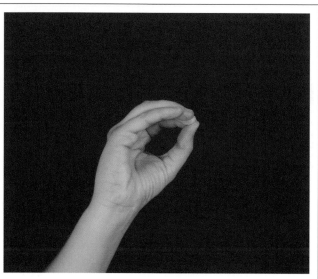

- The letter *o* mimics the shape of the written *o*.

- Simply close the fingers to the thumb.

- Curve the palm so it makes a round shape.

- The fingers and thumb will face the person you are talking to.

The Letter P

Does *p* look familiar? It is an upside-down *k*.

- The letter *p* can be a bit confusing at first.

- You will use three fingers: thumb, index, and middle finger.

- Keep the other two fingers folded down.

- The thumb will be resting between the index and middle fingers. Angle your wrist to be on top of the fingers.

ZOOM

Ever wonder how to attract a deaf person's attention? You can't yell "hey" across the room, clear your throat, or whistle. So, what's the best way to get a deaf person's? Use the lights! It is customary to flicker the lights on and off when you enter the room to alert the person you are there or to attract attention. Or, if you are across the room but have something to say, you can flicker the lights to grab her attention quickly. Inside or outside a wave is always a good way to indicate to a person that you have something to say.

If you are standing beside or near a deaf person, it is polite to lightly tap the person on the arm or shoulder. Whatever you do, be polite, wait a moment or two for a response before tapping again, and don't be overzealous with your tapping. You don't want to give the person a bruise! If the person is engaged in conversation with someone else, wait for a pause in signing before tapping. Or wait for the person to turn to you, giving you a chance to speak.

The Letter Q

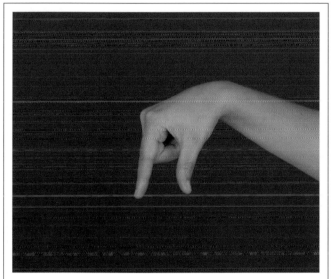

- Did you have trouble with the letter *g*? If not, *q* should be simple, too.

- Form the letter *q* using the thumb and index finger.

- Point the thumb and index finger down toward the ground.

The letter R

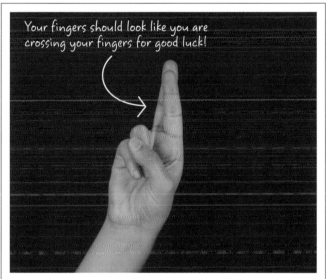

Your fingers should look like you are crossing your fingers for good luck!

- *R* uses the index and middle fingers.

- The other three fingers should be folded down. The thumb will cross over and rest on the folded fingers.

- Cross the middle finger over the index finger.

S, T, U, & V

Easy finger flow and proper formation make your letters easy to read

Although you might not expect it, even inside America various forms of sign language are used. You are learning American Sign Language, a true language, the language spoken within the Deaf community. American Sign Language, the primary language of the Deaf, is efficient in communicating ideas through body language, expression, and signs. ASL does not mirror the grammatical rules of English but is a true foreign language with its own verb, language, and syntax usage. ASL was first recognized as a true language in 1960 through the efforts of Dr. William Stokoe.

However, there are other types of sign language. Whereas ASL focuses on conveying the overall intent, others use Signed Exact English, which signs every word in exact translation to the spoken or written English. Luckily for you, ASL does not take as many signs to convey the same meaning, allowing you to ease into conversation with greater speed.

The Letter S

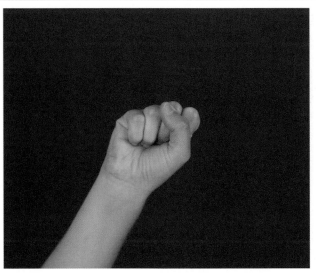

- The letters *s* and *a* can get a bit confusing.

- Unlike the *a*, where the thumb rests securely at the side of the fist, the letter *s* makes the same shape, but the thumb rests in front of the fingers.

- The shape resembles a tightly closed fist.

The Letter T

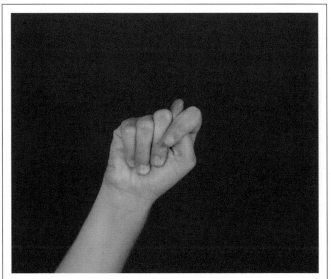

- Place the thumb underneath the index finger.

- Watch the finger placement to be sure you aren't saying *n* or *m*.

Who uses ASL? Although obviously the Deaf are the primary and most avid users of ASL, many other people in the community use ASL. Teachers and educators have long seen the value of teaching the youngest children and special needs children sign language. Policemen, social workers, ministry leaders, and children of deaf adults (CODAs) use ASL in their daily interactions.

ZOOM

Other Forms of Sign Language: Contact Signing is a bridge between ASL and Signed Exact English, borrowing signs from both, and is often used by educators and hearing people just learning sign. Signed Exact English incorporates the backbone of ASL but uses verb tenses, endings, prefixes, and suffixes. There is a one-to-one correspondence between spoken and signed English.

The Letter U

- *U* looks somewhat like the written u with the index and middle fingers extended upward.

- Unlike the written u, there is no space between the fingers. Be sure your fingers are pressed into one another.

The Letter V

- Like the letter *u* extend the index and middle fingers upward.

- Bring the fingers apart so that they make the *v* shape.

- The American Manual Alphabet *v* looks much like the written v.

11

W, X, Y, & Z

Congratulations! You are now equipped with all the letters of the alphabet

You've made it to the home stretch! With just a little bit of practice you'll be zipping through the American Manual Alphabet with ease and speed. Erase the "I can't" mentality and replace it with the "I can" as you master each new letter and sign. As with any sport, hobby, or skill, what you get out of ASL is largely determined by what you put into it. The more

time, effort, and energy you expend, the more of a working language you will gain. If you invest in classes and seek out opportunities to communicate with the Deaf, you'll find fluency in sign much more easily and quickly. As you engage with the Deaf around you, be prepared to explain your interest in sign language. Do you have a friend or family member

The Letter W

The letter w and the number 6 share the same sign.

- Just as in the English language, some words are spelled and pronounced the same but have multiple meanings (homonyms); the same is true with signs.

- The sign for *w* happens to be one of those signs. In popular culture, this sign means 3, but in ASL, the sign for *w* is

also the sign for *6*.

- When you see this sign being used, be sure to remember the dual meanings and check the context clues for which meaning the speaker is intending.

- Form *w* by extending the index, middle, and ring fingers.

The Letter X

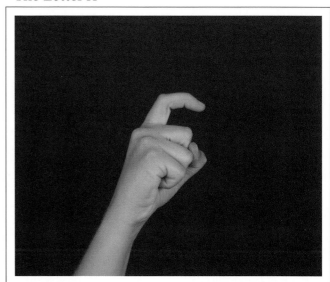

- As you've noticed, the letter *x* is formed with a tight fist except for the index finger.

- Make sure your index finger is tight and not loose.

- Use a little finger muscle to create the sharp bend of the finger, forming almost a boxlike shape.

- If your fingers are flaccid, the shape won't make sense.

who is deaf? Or do you have just an interest in the beauty of the language? Don't hesitate to really use the resource guide in Chapter 20 to dive into the Deaf community.

The syntax order, the exclusion of all words, and body language are going to be the biggest differences between English and ASL for a new signer. Spending time with the deaf will help you to understand these differences and to implement your own signing style. You've already made a huge step by learning the alphabet. You have the tools to begin a conversation, say your name, and get to know a new person. Feel proud of your accomplishment!

Keep your lines straight and the size of the z proportionate.

The Letter Y

- *Y* is straightforward and simple, with an easy extension of the thumb and pinky finger.

- The closed fingers will be facing the person you are talking to.

- Remember to hold your hand still.

The Letter Z

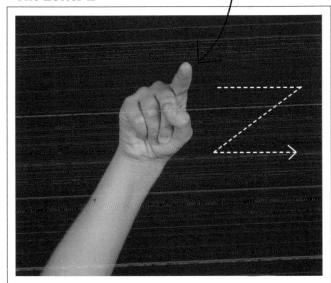

- Using your second finger as your marker, write the letter *z* on the board in front of you.

- Although it is fun, try not to overly zigzag the *z*, making it hard to read for the person you are speaking to.

- *Z* is the most fun letter in the alphabet and may be the easiest for novices to remember.

1, 2, 3, & 4
Counting with your fingers is as easy as 1, 2, 3

Now that you're tackling numbers, you can see immediately that you already know some of these signs. You've probably been saying 1, 2, 3 your whole life and been counting on your hands since kindergarten. Counting on your hands in ASL looks a little different than what you are used to. For example, what you will notice immediately is that the way you've been saying *3* may look a little different in sign language. Why? Well, because the way you're used to saying 3

means both *w* and *6*. Confusing? Consider adding "3" to the meaning, too. You get the point. So, rather than having the *3* sign convey three meanings, it is much simpler to say *3* the same way you would say *2* but extending your thumb at the same time. See, now, this can't possibly mean anything other than 3. It will feel uncomfortable at first, especially because this isn't the way you are used to saying 3. Practice signing *1, 2, 3,* and your new version of "3" will be routine in no time.

Number 1

- The number *1* is how you've been saying 1 your whole life.

- Simply extend the index finger straight in the air. The finger should not be bent or crooked.

- Close the remaining fingers together in an o like shape.

Number 2

When signing, be sure you take care in your form and execution.

- Form the number *2* just as you have always done when counting on your hands.

- The number *2* is the same sign as for the letter *v*.

- Only the index and middle finger will be extended. All other fingers will be closed in an o like shape.

You'll notice that *1, 2, 4,* and *5* are how you've always counted on your fingers. See how much you already know? It gets a little trickier from *6* on.

Notice the firm grasp of the palm and the rigid finger making the number *1.* When signing numbers, letters, or signs, taking care with your execution is much like making sure you don't mumble sounds.

Do your best to keep those fourth and pinky fingers closed.

Number 3

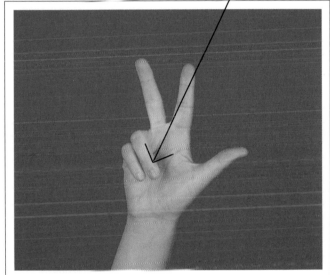

- The number *3* is signed differently than how it is signed in popular culture.

- Much like the number *2,* the number *3* extends the index and middle finger. It also adds the extension of the thumb.

- The ring and pinky fingers fold downward. There should be spaces between the extended fingers.

- Avoid confusing the popular culture *3* with the signed number *3.* Otherwise you'll be signing *6* instead of *3.*

Number 4

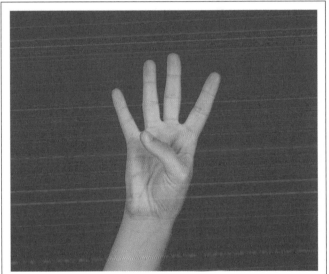

- We're returning to your comfort zone with the signed number *4.* Sign *4* just as popular culture does.

- All fingers except the thumb will be extended. Keep your fingers straight and spaced apart.

15

5, 6, 7, & 8

Who do we appreciate? *You!* Congratulate yourself for learning a new language

Is learning ASL numbers really that important? Yes! Consider all the applications you use numbers for in everyday life. Age, address, telephone number, account numbers, student ID numbers, driver's license numbers, how many in a party, how many minutes to go, time, and date are just a sampling of the many applications you need numbers for. Saying numbers

in ASL is a basic building block you need to learn. You'll find that the succession of numbers is often logical ands make sense. After you begin a pattern, you'll pick up the series in no time.

To indicate that something is first, second, third, fourth or more, begin by forming the number. Then twist the wrist to-

Number 5

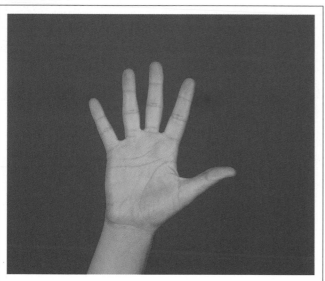

- Already know this sign? You'll be glad to know you already have some signs in your vocabulary like *5* and *you.*

- The number *5* is made using an open palm with all five fingers extended.

Number 6

- The number 6 is where the numbers begin to change from what you have typically used in counting.

- Form *6* by drawing your thumb and pinky finger together. The middle three fingers will be extended straight.

- There should be spaces between the fingers.

- The number *6* is the same sign as the letter *w.*

ward your body. This indicates a rank order.

If you are indicating the time of an event or appointment, first say the sign time by tapping your wrist with the dominant index finger. So, to say 7:30 you would first say *time* and then sign *7* and *30*.

After you have the number basics down, practice signing your phone number, your address (first the numbers, then finger spell the street location), and ages of your children. These are questions that you are bound to answer in conversation, so practice the answers now!

Number 7

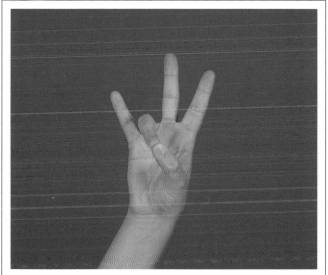

- The numbers all follow a logical succession.

- The number 7 follows after 6 but uses the fourth finger (instead of the pinky) to meet the thumb.

- All other fingers are extended straight.

Number 8

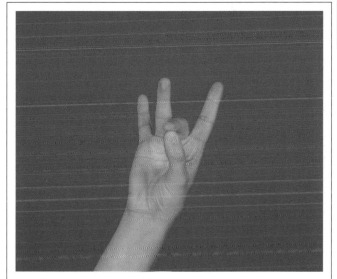

- Following in the same progression as 6 and 7, the middle finger comes down and meets the thumb.

- All other fingers are extended outward.

- Practice starting from 5 and quickly change from the pinky all the way to the middle finger, and you'll see how logically and easily you can say 6, 7, and 8 all with one hand!

9, 10, 11, & 12
Double-digit counting all with a single hand

If you are the only hearing person in the room, should you use your voice? The choice is up to you. Speaking or mouthing your words will help those Deaf who can speech read, whereas it may detract from the understanding of those who do not.

The person you are speaking to may or may not use her voice to talk back with you. If the person does use her voice, it probably won't sound the same as a hearing person's voice for several reasons. If the person lost her hearing later in life,

her verbal skills are usually strong and clear. Persons born profoundly deaf have never heard their voice and therefore must learn how to find and use their voice. Once the voice is discovered, the person must then learn how to pair the voice to word lip movements. Factors such the person's age at time of voice awareness, how much therapy and training the person received, and how much the person uses his voice all affect speech clarity.

Number 9

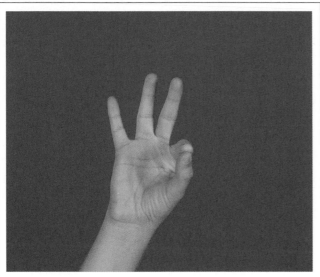

- After *8* logically comes *9*. Much like *6, 7,* and *8,* the sign for *9* follows the same fashion by having the pointer finger and thumb join.
- The number *9* is the same sign as the letter *f.*

Number 10

- The number *10* finishes off the succession with a simple flick of the wrist.
- Twist your dominant wrist outward to say *10.*

The more you are around the Deaf, the more easily you will be able to understand their voices. Don't be surprised if the Deaf may be very loud or excessively quiet. Because they can't hear themselves, they have no internal sense of the right range of volume control. Feel free to give them some indication if they are too loud or too quiet for a situation. Many Deaf, especially those who were educated with the oral method (no use of ASL), are able to speak and engage in conversation with great ease.

Number 11

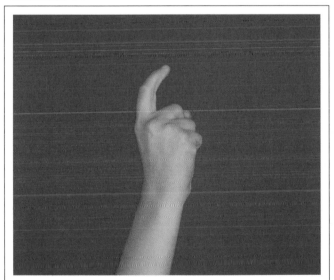

- The number *11* goes back to the use of fingers in succession.

- Instead of meeting the thumb with fingers, the numbers *11* through *19* employ more of a flicking motion.

- The number *11* is made by having your hand in a fist-like motion with the nail of your pointer finger just inside your thumb and quickly flicking out.

Number 12

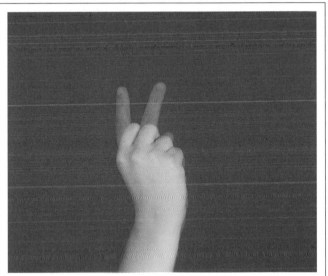

- The number *12* is made much the same way as *11* but using both your middle finger and pointer finger.

- Bring both the middle and pointer fingers to your thumb and then quickly flick forward.

19

13, 14, 15, & 16
Feeling a little thumb tied? Shake those fingers and try again

CODAs learn these ABC and 1, 2, 3 basics as any other child would learn the alphabet. As a CODA, I took it upon myself to teach my friends the alphabet and numbers. It was a great tool for talking when teachers assigned us to different lunch tables. I was the recess entertainment as kids clocked my ABC speed. They were amazed at how fast my fingers could go from *a* to *z*—much faster than I ever could have spoken it.

Growing up, speaking ASL was as natural as talking. A ques-tion asked of me over and over again as a CODA was "How did you learn how to talk?" I never really found a good answer to that question. How does anyone learn to talk? We are a product of our surroundings. We learn what we hear and what we see. My sister and I both signed and spoke. My parents both used their voices constantly while they spoke through sign. My grandparents, who were both hearing, were constants in our lives.

Number 13

- The number *13* uses the number *3* with a twist. Turn your palm facing yourself so that you are staring at the number *3*.

- Now bring the two fingers (middle and pointer) in a back-and-forth motion about two times.

Number 14

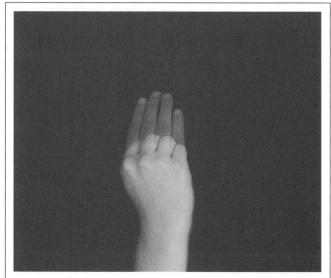

- The number *14* is similar. Make the number *4* with palm facing you.

- Fold forward and back the four fingers (not your thumb) over your thumb about two times in a quick back-and-forth motion.

- This makes the number *14*.

- This is not a slow motion. Be quick! The motion should be done about twice in a single second.

Life as a CODA: Other questions we heard growing up included, "Will your kids be deaf?" Although I wasn't certain of that answer, I wasn't afraid to have deaf children, knowing they could live full lives. But my husband and I have four beautiful, completely hearing children. "Can the Deaf have children?" Hello? Wasn't talking to me the answer to that question? And last, "Can your sister hear?" My sister and I were both born completely hearing, although my mom and my aunt are both deaf. Many deaf parents may have one hearing and one deaf child.

For my sister and me, deafness was as normal and natural as hearing. Although we had a few more flashing lights, and we interpreted for our parents, we gained the benefit of being a part of the Deaf community.

Number 15

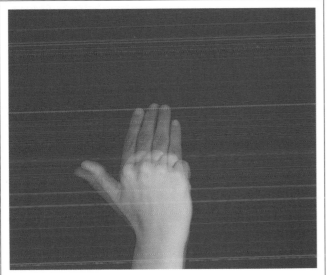

- To say *15*, do the same thing as *14* but stick your thumb out.

- You'll be making a *5* palm facing toward yourself, taking the four fingers again (not your thumb) in the same quick back-and-forth motion.

Number 16

- The number *16* deviates from the pattern you've had for *13*, *14*, and *15*.

- Begin with your hand in the letter *a* position. Next, form the number *6*, or letter *w*.

- Quickly move your pinky finger in a back-and-forth motion over the thumb.

21

17, 18, 19, & 20

Counting to 20 in a new language has never been so easy

In two short chapters you have learned how to master the Manual American Alphabet as well as count to 20. Just think of the conversations you can have now!

The next step is action. What are you going to do with all this knowledge? Does it do anyone any good if you only practice in your bathroom occasionally? If you are going to go to the trouble to learn the language, then don't be shy about using it. Find people in church, school, or in clubs in your community. Make the effort to find them and begin to use your new signing skills.

Yeah, at first it might be awkward. Your fingers will feel weird and twisted. You'll second guess the signs you are making. You'll marvel at the speed, intensity, and expression of those who are fluent in ASL. Undoubtedly there will be moments when you won't know what is being said. Don't let the ASL accomplished discourage you from trying. It's perfectly nor-

Number 17

- If you mastered the number *16*, you'll have no trouble at all with *17*, *18*, and *19*.

- Starting with *17* you'll begin using your fourth, or ring, finger to cross over the thumb in a back-and-forth motion.

Number 18

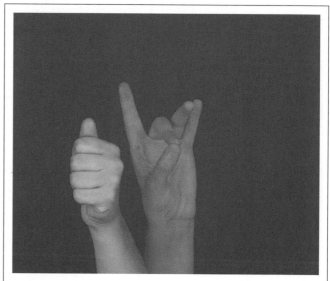

- The number *18* uses the same pattern but with the middle finger. Cross the middle finger over the thumb.

- Move your fingers in a back-and-forth motion.

mal and natural to feel all of these things. Every beginner has to start somewhere. You don't have to be perfect, just willing and able to learn from your mistakes. If you never take the chance, you'll never know where this new language journey could have taken you. Take a chance on a new language. Take a chance on getting to know a new culture. You'll be glad you did.

Number 19

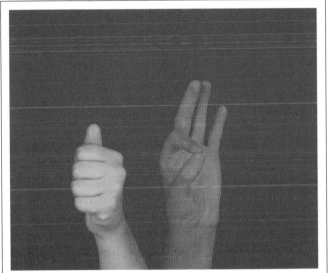

- Forming *19* is essentially the same as forming the number *9*, but with a brush. Brush the index finger back and forth against the thumb.

- The remaining fingers will remain extended

- Now that you're seeing the pattern emerge, you're probably able to better remember the pattern.

Number 20

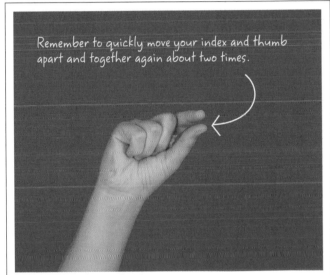

Remember to quickly move your index and thumb apart and together again about two times.

- The succession of fingers follows in a logical direction indicating one number going up or down.

- The number *20* breaks the rhythm. Form *20* by bringing your second, or pointer, finger down onto the thumb and move it back and forth.

- The other fingers in your hand will remain in a closed-fist position. The thumb and the pointer finger moving back and forth resemble a bird pecking.

30, 40, 50, & 60
Count by tens with speed and agility

Have you ever been in a church and watched a person sign a song? Watching the hands move in time to the music is mesmerizing. The signer looks as though she is completely one with the signs, the music, and the meanings of the words. One of the hallmarks of ASL is how the meanings of the words are integrated into the signs. When you speak the words, your body expression shows that it feels it. This active, vibrant language is exciting, always interesting, and fluid. When you

engage in an ASL conversation you don't ever have to worry about being bored. There is enough emotion, activity, and movement to pique and hold your interest. This beautiful language is active. To speak in ASL is to become joined with the words and their meanings.

You may not think that a number can evoke much emotion. Yet, what if a deaf person needs to call 911? The sense of urgency would be apparent as the numbers *911* were signed.

Number 30

- The number *30* is formed by first forming the number *3*. The thumb will be extended and the index and middle fingers extended straight.

- After forming the *3* quickly bring in those three fingers to form a *0* shape while your ring finger and your pinky finger remain closed in.

Number 40

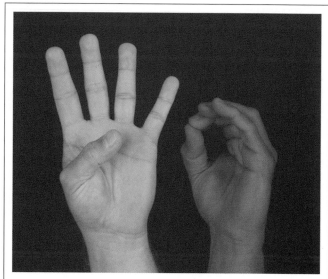

- The number *40* begins with the number *4*. The thumb will be folded over the palm with the four fingers extended straight.

- Next, quickly bring in the four extended fingers to form a *0* while the thumb remains tucked in.

What if you were describing a wait at a local restaurant as more than an hour? Your face would look irritated and upset that the wait was so long. Even with numbers you will find a strong emotional tie to the signs.

To form the numbers *30, 40, 50,* and *60,* you will see yet another pattern emerging. Each number is essentially two signs, quickly blending into one. You'll begin with the first part of the *3, 4,* or *5* and then make the *0* shape.

Number 50

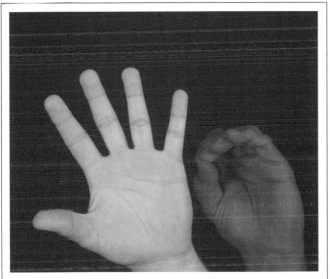

- The number *50,* because it starts with a *5,* will use all five fingers.

- First form the number *5.*

- Next, form the letter *o* or number *0* by bringing all five fingers together.

Number 60

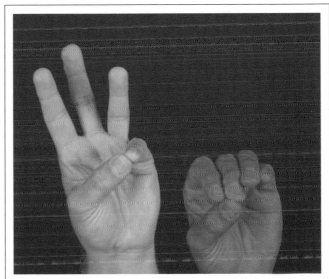

- The number *60* begins with the number *6.* The middle three fingers will be extended straight while the pinky and thumb meet.

- Quickly fold down the extended fingers to form the *o* shape.

- Notice that the fingers forming the second part of the sign are always the fingers extended when making the initial number. Don't make the sign harder than it is by trying to also use the fingers that are closed.

70, 80, 90, & 100
You've learned counting by tens through 100

Although not all deaf persons speech read (also known as "lip reading"), many do. So, it is helpful when you sign to look directly at the person and to speak the words as you sign. Be careful not to mumble, mutter, or speak with a strong accent if possible. If a deaf person can't quite understand your signs, she can often pair your speech movements with your hand movements to understand with more accuracy what you are trying to say.

Now that you have the knowledge, practice counting by tens through 100. After you've mastered counting by tens, begin practicing other numbers—age, amounts of checks or bills—any numbers used around you will work. Perfect practice makes a difference. As you can see, *70, 80,* and *90* are also formed in the same pattern as *30, 40, 50,* and *60.*

Number 70

- Begin *70* with forming the number *7* with the ring finger touching the thumb, all other fingers extended.
- After forming the *7*, bring all fingers down to a closed-fist position.

Number 80

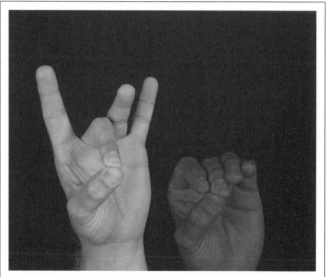

- The number *80* begins with making the number *8* with the middle finger touching the thumb.
- Next, bring all fingers down to form an *o.*

"It's not important." This phrase is heard all too often by deaf persons who ask a hearing person what was just said. To the hearing person, the information may have been insignificant, useless chatter, but that person has just made the decision of what is important to hear and what isn't. The Deaf want to hear all of the information and have the ability to decide what is important and not.

Sure, many times something that is said may not be important, but not going to the trouble to tell what was just stated makes the deaf person feel left out and ignored. Ask yourself how you would feel; talk to and include the deaf person as much as possible. The deaf person may agree—what was said wasn't important—but he'll also agree that you giving him the chance to make that decision was very important.

Number 90

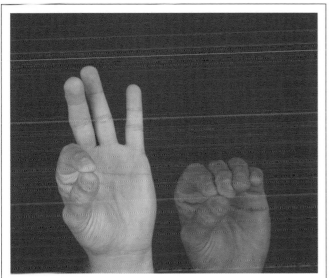

- First form the number *9* touching the index finger and thumb together. All remaining fingers are extended.

- Next, bring all fingers down to form an *o*.

Number 100

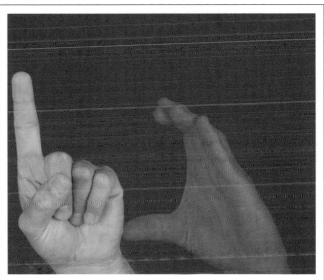

- The number *100* is a two-part sign.

- The first part begins with a single-digit number. For example, to say *100*, begin

with the number *1*.

- Next, form the letter *c*. So, *100* would look like *1 c*.

COUNTING BIG
Big numbers mean a big impact, all with just one hand

Counting in larger numerations is not difficult at all. Now that you've mastered other numbers you will use that foundation for the larger numbers. Here we will focus on learning *thousand, hundred thousand*, and *million*. You can use other numbers you have learned to form mixed denominations.

Many Deaf refer to their peer group as the "Deaf family" for a number of reasons. If a person is the only deaf person in a home, holidays and other social gatherings are often a time where he feels largely alone and left out while the rest of the family laughs, talks, and engages in conversation. With his deaf peers he has people who know exactly what life feels like for him, who talk and communicate the same way he does, and who place a high value on knowing all they can about the other person. When saying hello and goodbye, warm hugs and long, drawn-out goodbyes are not uncommon. Often their friends have been a part of their peer group

Thousand

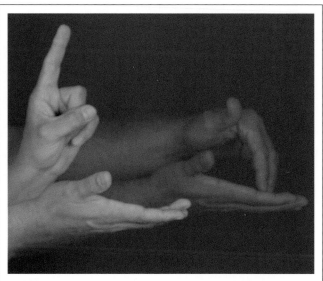

- The stationary or passive hand will be in a flat, palm-up position.

- The dominant hand will strike against the passive hand.

- As pictured, if you wanted to say *1,000*, first form the number *1* and then the *thousand* sign. If you wanted to say *7,000*, start instead with the number *7* and then the *thousand* sign.

Hundred Thousand

- To form a number in the hundred thousand range, you will use a combination of three signs, all signs you have already learned.

- For example, to say *300,000*, begin with *3*. Next say *hundred* and lastly say *thousand*.

since they were small children and have literally known each other their whole lives. Sadly, many Deaf find themselves feeling much closer to their "Deaf family" than their blood family. Knowing how the Deaf interact, which can be as simple as counting numbers with your deaf friend, will help you as you forge new friendships within this loving family.

Million is a large number. Is your face reflecting it? Remember to facially express your words.

Million

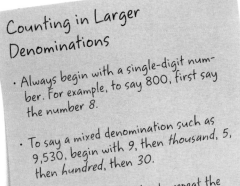

- The difference between *million* and *thousand* is just one extra step.

- Simply add another striking of the fingertips against the palm about 2 or 3 inches higher.

- To say *5,000,000* you will (1) make a *5*, (2) sign *thousand*, and (3) add another strike against the palm several inches higher.

MAKE IT EASY

Don't leave a social setting without saying a face-to-face "goodbye." In a hearing world a "goodbye" can be heard from the doorway or across the room. When you have a deaf friend it is important to individually say "goodbye." If you leave without letting your friend know it, you will seem very rude.

Counting in Larger Denominations

- Always begin with a single-digit number. For example, to say 800, first say the number 8.

- To say a mixed denomination such as 9,530, begin with 9, then *thousand*, 5, then *hundred*, then 30.

- It's always a good idea to repeat the number a few times to be sure no mistake has been made in either speaking or understanding the number.

RAINBOW COLORS
Add some color to your signing vocabulary

Let's get back to the basics. Red, yellow, blue, and green are some core colors that every signer should know. Colors add drama, beauty, and visual stimulation to your world. Learning the words for these colors will help you add a bit of detail to your signing repertoire.

The signs for colors tend to use the first letter of the color being signed. But this isn't always the case. Some colors are also signed around the face: Pink and red are formed near the lips, associating red with the lips. Black is formed over the eyebrows, just as eyebrows are usually a dark color. Brown is on the side of the face, and orange is just over the lips.

Other signs use a back-and-forth shaking motion in conjunction with the first letter of their name. Those colors are yellow, green, blue, and purple.

Use colors to describe life around you. Clothes, food, shoes, stores, paint, eyes, and more can all be described using color.

Red

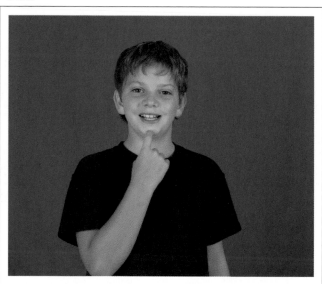

- Place the index finger of your dominant hand to the bottom of your chin.

- Lightly brush the index finger about two times in a downward motion.

- An alternate verion of *red* involves forming the letter *r* and placing the *r* just above the lips. Like the sign shown, brush the *r* in a downward motion about two times.

Yellow

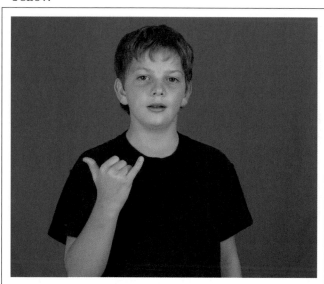

- Form the letter *y* with your dominant hand with the pinky and thumb extended.

- Twist your wrist back and forth to say *yellow*.

These colors are also great signs to use in combination with words for babies and toddlers and signs in the classroom. Children of all ages use color every day in the classroom. Don't be afraid to add color to your vocabulary!

Blue and green are good examples of the types of color signs that use the shaking of the letter back and forth.

⋯⋯⋯⋯⋯⋯ GREEN ● LIGHT ⋯⋯⋯⋯⋯⋯

Want more practice? First finger spell the color and then follow it up with the color's sign. Try to name the color of objects in your home or neighborhood. Practicing both finger spelling and signing will increase your speed, accuracy, and sign fluency.

Blue

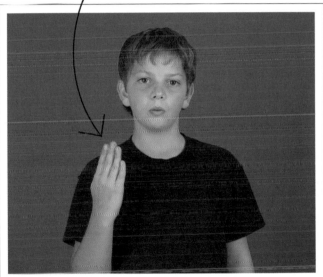

- The dominant hand will form the letter *b* with the four fingers extended and thumb folded over the palm.

- Twist the wrist back and forth to say *blue*.

Green

- *Green* is made forming the letter *g* with the dominant hand. *G* uses the index and middle fingers horizontally extended.

- Twist the wrist back and forth to say *green*.

MORE COLORS

Whether a blazing orange or a pretty purple, get to know your colors

When learning your colors, remember that when you meet a deaf person, you'll often notice that her other senses are acute and tend to fill in for the lost sense of hearing. The deaf person has enhanced sensitivity to a variety of things. For example, hearing is often felt through vibrations. The Deaf can feel a train coming, know when music is too loud, or feel the bass from a loud speaker. Many Deaf also have a sense of smell far keener than that of a person with full hearing.

Many odors that would not bother a hearing person, such as certain foods or a perfume, may be too strong, offensive, or overwhelming. The Deaf also tend to have great memorization skills, having honed them through learning how to read and understand English, both tasks that normally rely on hearing sounds. The Deaf also have a heightened sense of body language awareness. They will pick up subtle messages of interest or boredom, friendliness, or rudeness. Knowing

Orange

- Depending on whom you speak to and where you live, the color orange may or may not use the letter *o* in the sign.

- Some sign *orange* instead with the use of their pinky

fingers. To say *orange* this way, swirl the pinky fingers around each other, without touching.

- Above you see *orange* as a color or fruit. Squeeze the letter *o* around your lips.

Purple

- *Purple* is formed by making the letter *p* with the dominant hand. Remember that the thumb is tucked neatly between the thumb and the index finger. The

wrist is turned so that the fingers are extended below the wrist.

- Move the *p* back and forth in a side-to-side motion.

this, it is important to be mindful of where your eyes are looking. Don't have wandering eyes, and have a look of interest on your face. Colors and their influence in the world around them play an important role in their sense of awareness.

White symbolizes purity and innocence. If using white in this context, reflect it with your face.

········ YELLOW ●LIGHT ········

Depending on whom you talk to and what region you live in, you may have two signs for *orange:* one sign for the fruit orange and one sign for the color orange. For these people, the signs are not synonymous. The sign of the fruit orange is made by squeezing the letter *o* around your lips, almost as if you were squeezing an orange for juice.

Pink

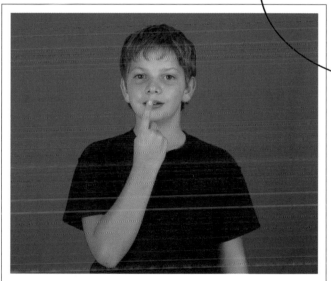

- *Pink* uses the letter *p* also.

- Place the *p* right above the lip and brush it downward several times.

White

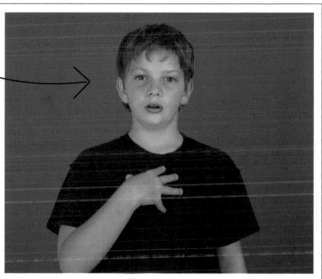

- White is another color that does not use the beginning letter in the sign.

- Begin with the open palm of the dominant hand spread out across the top of the chest.

- As you pull your hand away from your body, close the fingers together to form *white*.

DEFINE WITH COLOR
How light? How dark? Add dramatic definition with color

Let's finish out colors with black, brown, light, and dark. These colors tend to really add drama to a situation. Black is symbolic of something fearful, dark, and scary. Light and dark are great tools to describe a shade of a color, the weather outside, weight, and more.

Light and dark are two perfect examples of how facial expression is used in sign language. Notice that when the person is signing *light*, the face looks uplifted, cheery, and bright. Contrast that expression to *dark*, where the expression is somber and sad. These emotional physical expressions are as important as the motions with your hands.

As you learn more signs, refer back to these pages to add color to the description. As much as you can, try to make two- and three-word combinations. The more you practice signing phrases, the easier it will be to do when you need to. Add numbers to the phrases to indicate how many of something.

Black

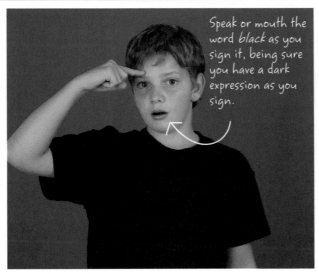

Speak or mouth the word *black* as you sign it, being sure you have a dark expression as you sign.

- Form the number *1* with your dominant hand.

- Horizontally place the *1* above your forehead.

- Move your *1* across the length of the brow.

Brown

- *Brown* begins with the letter *b*.

- Beginning at the top of your forehead, near your temple, draw down the *b* toward your chin.

34

Now you've mastered the building block basics, and you're ready to move on and learn signs for situations and the world around you. Go color your world!

Light

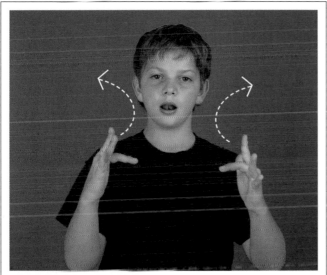

- *Light* is made using both hands.

- With both palms somewhat opened, draw your middle finger slightly down.

- Holding both hands out in front of you just above waist level, begin with the thumbs facing each other.

- Then move your hands until the thumbs face upward.

Dark

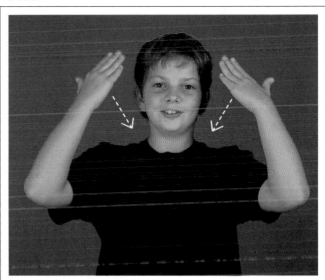

- *Dark* uses both hands.

- Begin with the fingers on each hand together, palm facing your body.

- Begin with both hands about 6 inches from either side of your face.

- Cross your hands across your face making an x with your hands.

35

ASKING QUESTIONS
Who? What? Why? Be in the know and know how to ask

Who, what, and why are basic questions in any language. Let's get started on asking these questions. Keep in mind the question you are asking and be sure your facial expression is reflecting the question. Your facial expression is the inflection in the voice indicating to the person you are asking a question.

On these two pages you will learn the signs who, what, and why (as pictured). You may also want to know how to say the word *which*, made with each hand making the thumbs-up sign. Moving at the same time in opposite directions, move the fists up and down, thumbs facing up, to say *which*.

As you sign the word *who* be sure to say the word at the same time. You'll find that many signs have more than one way of saying them. *Who* can be said using your index finger will be facing your mouth circling the mouth. Or sign *who* as described and pictured below.

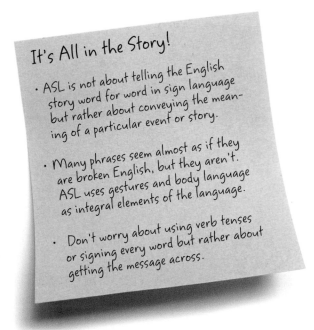

It's All in the Story!

- ASL is not about telling the English story word for word in sign language but rather about conveying the meaning of a particular event or story.

- Many phrases seem almost as if they are broken English, but they aren't. ASL uses gestures and body language as integral elements of the language.

- Don't worry about using verb tenses or signing every word but rather about getting the message across.

Who?

- Begin with the letter *x*. Remember that *x* is formed using your index finger, bent at both knuckles.

- Place the *x* perpendicular to your lips. Do not place the *x* on top of your lips but rather about 1 inch away.

- Move the index finger back and forth slightly two to three times.

- Say *who?* as you sign the word and be sure your face mirrors the question being asked.

What's new? is a simple two-word phrase you can use as a quick conversation starter. To say *new* you will use the stationary hand in an open-palm position facing upward. Cup your dominant hand in a *c* position. Brush the backside of the *c* against the open palm of the stationary hand. Have a quizzical expression asking the person what is new in his life.

What?

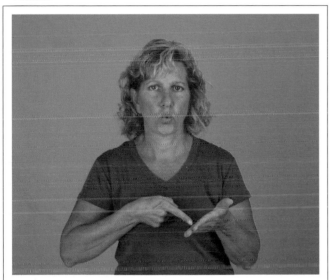

- The index finger of your dominant hand will strike the stationary hand.

- Strike the index finger quickly against the palm.

- The stationary hand will be in a nonmoving, open-palm position.

- Your eyes and face should look somewhat confused because you don't know the answer to this *what* question.

- Consider which words you want to pair with *what* to form questions. Time? Eat? Combining words will form questions.

Why?

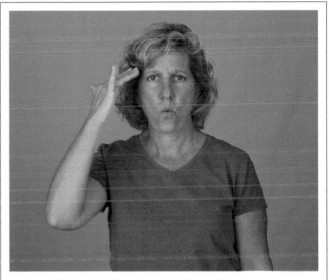

- Place the dominant hand fingertips on the forehead, in between the eyebrows, or just above the eyebrows.

- Draw your hand away from your head and form the letter *y* (thumb and pinky finger extended with the three middle fingers closed).

- The *y* will be facing your body instead of your speaking partner.

- Is your face asking the question *why*? Practice in front of a mirror and see if your facial expressions match the question being asked.

BUILDING BLOCKS

YOURS, MINE, & OURS
Whose is it, yours or mine? Learn to answer that important question

You'll be relieved to see that *you* is just as you have been saying it your whole life. Simply point your finger at the person to indicate the word *you*. Other signs that you probably already know or say in a version close to the ASL sign are the numbers *1, 2, 4,* and *5*. *My, look, crown*, and *hat* are other words that are probably what you would sign even without being taught ASL.

Many signs form off of one another. If you were to take the same *mine* motion and angle it slightly off center toward the right or left, the sign would then mean *his* or *hers,* and if you took it even farther to the right or left, the sign would then mean *theirs*. Accuracy is important to ensure you are saying the words you mean to say.

To say something is *his* you will form the sign for *boy* and then point as though you are pointing to someone. To say something is *hers* you will form the *girl* sign and point as

You

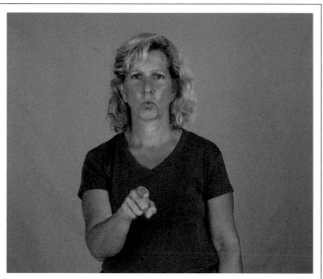

- Point your finger outward.

- Say or mouth the word *you* as you point.

- Make eye contact with the person you are speaking to.

Yours

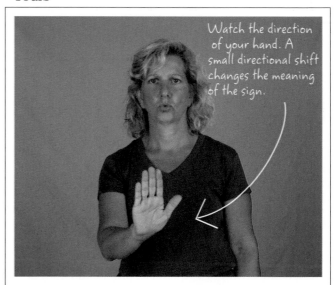

Watch the direction of your hand. A small directional shift changes the meaning of the sign.

- Begin with the letter *b* sign, but with the thumb extended outward. The fingers will not have spaces between them.

- Your elbow will first be bent; as you push the palm outward, your elbow will

extend directly toward the person you are speaking to.

- Don't do anything with the other hand. Leave it at rest at your side.

- Say or mouth the word *yours* as you make the sign.

though you are pointing to someone.

To describe someone or something with greater emphasis, finger spell the word clearly. For example, if you want to say *wow*, spell out *w-o-w* or, to describe an especially pretty person, you can spell out *p-r-e-t-t-y*.

As you move your hand across your chest you will be forming a half-circle.

Mine

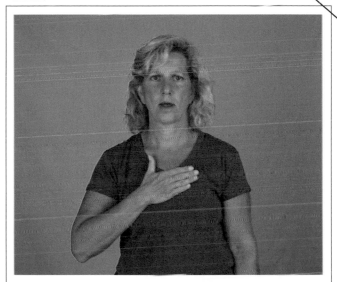

- Make the same open-thumb *b* position as used in *yours*.

- Place the palm against your chest.

- Say or mouth the word *mine* as you sign it.

- Remember how a three-year-old says mine with all of her body and face? Your facial expression should be that expressive, indicating that whatever you are talking about is undoubtedly owned by you. Don't worry about overexaggeration.

Our

- Slightly cup your dominant hand. The fingers will be together with no spaces.

- Place the cupped hand on the same shoulder as the hand you are signing with. If you are right handed, you'll begin with your right shoulder.

- Move the hand to the other shoulder in an arc like motion.

- Say or mouth the word *our* or *ours* as you sign the word.

BUILDING BLOCKS

TELL ME . . .

Can I? Where is it? How come? Know how to sign questions that matter

When you are in a group setting with a deaf person or a group of deaf people, be sensitive to including them in the conversation. The Deaf often feel excluded because conversations often are not aimed at them or are not translated in full. Sometimes, the Deaf are given just a synopsis of what is discussed. The Deaf will ask many questions because they want to understand what is being discussed and to be sure that no details are being left out. They can't overhear little tidbits from others around them or even what is happening on the evening news as they use their eyes to prepare dinner. So, they make the most of every opportunity to hear through their hands.

Can?

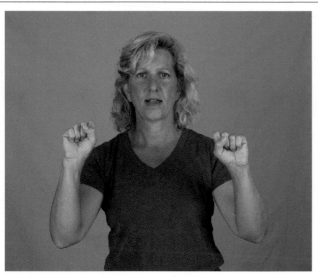

- Form two closed fists and place them at chest level. Thumbs will be tucked tightly to the fist.

- Move both fists downward simultaneously until you reach about waist level.

- Don't move too quickly or slowly, but at a medium speed.

- Ask a question with your expression, as well as saying or mouthing the word *can* as you sign.

Where?

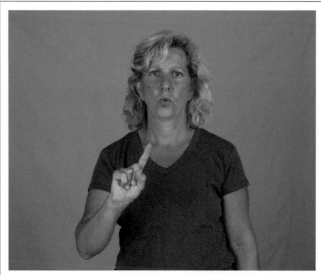

- *Where* is a one-handed sign. You will use your dominant hand.

- Extend the index finger out keeping all other fingers in a closed fist.

- Move your index finger back and forth by shifting your wrist to the left and then to the right several times.

- Have your question face on. Speak or mouth the word *where* as you sign.

How can you include a deaf person in the conversation? Take a moment to sign or gesture to the person what has just been said. Give the person an opportunity to ask a question. Tell the others to wait a second before continuing conversation until the deaf person is caught up in the conversation. Always speak clearly so that, if the deaf person can speech read, many words will be understood as they are spoken.

Here we will learn *can, where, come,* and *how?* These all are words you'll need for this basic conversation.

How?

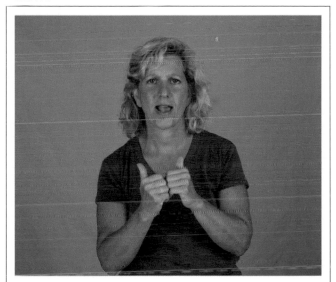

- *How* is a two-part sign. The first part will begin with both fists touching. The thumbs will be extended upward, while all other fingers are in a closed fist.

- The second part of the sign involves motion. Simultaneously move each fist away from each other.

- The final position of the sign will end with the thumbs pointing in opposite directions from one another.

- Again, your face should be asking a question, and your lips should be speaking or mouthing the word as you say it.

Come

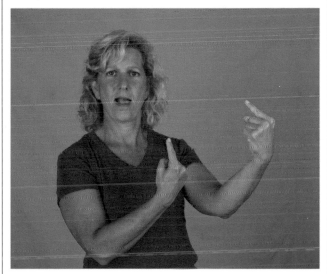

- *Come* is made using both hands forming the number *1.*

- Stretch your dominant arm out slightly higher than the stationary arm, which will be relatively close to your body.

- Draw together the dominant hand to the stationary hand, as though two things that are apart are now coming together.

ANSWERS
Know how to ask and answer questions—yes and no are just a start

You need to learn to sign *yes* and *no*? I'm kidding, right? Isn't *yes* said by shaking your head up and down and *no* by shaking your head side to side? Well, yes and no . . . Although, of course, saying yes and no in these ways is widely used in ASL, there is also a way to say yes and no using your hands. Here we will focus on the basic answers of *yes* and *no* as well as two forms of punctuation the Deaf often use in conversation: the period and the question mark.

Obviously yes and no won't be the only answers you'll need in your signing repertoire. Some other common answers are *true, OK, but, wait,* and *stay,* which are all simple signs that can be learned through description.

To say *true*, place your index finger against your chin. Move the finger away from your chin. To say *okay*, simply finger spell *o* and then *k*.

To say *but*, cross both index fingers over one another and

Yes

Shake your head yes or no while making the signs.

- Use your dominant hand and form the letter *s*.

- The fist will be closed with the thumb folded over the closed fingers.

- With your wrist, move your fist up and down.

- The up-and-down motion of the wrist mirrors the head nod of yes.

No

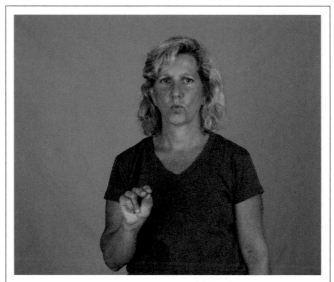

- *No* is a single-hand sign.

- You will use only three fingers: the thumb and the index and middle fingers.

- Begin with the index finger and middle finger touching, while the ring and pinky finger remain closed.

- Bring the index finger and middle finger to meet the thumb. Open and close the fingers again several times.

then spread them apart. To form *wait,* simply wiggle the fingers of each hand while the palms face your body. To form *stay,* form the letter *y* with your dominant hand. Move it downward about 2 inches and bring it to a halt, almost as if it has hit a shelf or counter. The fingers will be face down. Using these new signs you'll now have a wide range of responses.

Question Mark

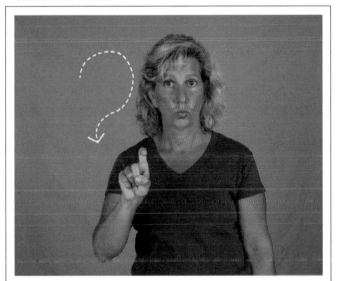

- ASL integrates the use of a question mark to indicate that a question is being asked.

- It is used in conversation much like writing a question mark at the end of written question.

- Much like the letter z, the question mark is made by drawing it on the space in front of you with your finger.

- Imagine a small chalk board directly in front of you. With your index finger draw a question mark.

Period

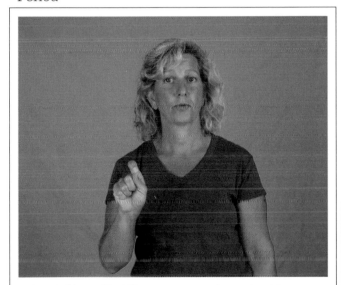

- A period is used in ASL to convey emphasis.

- If a person is very opinionated or if the answer is final and not subject to change, he will use the period sign.

- The period is made by the thumb and pointer finger

meeting and making a forceful dot or period in the space in front of you.

- The face will also have an emphatic expression, showing that the person is dead serious.

WHERE?

Learn the location basics—over, under, near, and far

With these next four signs you will learn ways to describe proximity or things in relation to one another. Pictured below are the four signs *over, under, near,* and *far*.

Proximity in time is also an important element. You will want to be able to describe if something happens after or before or when it begins. These simple signs can be quickly learned.

After is a simple two-part sign. Begin by placing each side-

ways facing palm to rest on top of one another in an x formation. After making the x move the dominant palm over the stationary palm.

Begin uses both hands. The stationary hand is flat, palm facing upwards. The dominant index finger tip rests on the palm and twists. *Before* also uses both hands. Begin with the dominant hand resting on top of the stationary hand. Move the dominant hand toward your body.

Over

- Begin *over* with both hands.

- The stationary hand will be in a flat, horizontal palm position. The palm will face downward toward the floor.

- The dominant hand will be in a horizontal palm

- position directly over the stationary hand.

- Move the dominant hand in a counterclockwise rotation. The moving hand is symbolic of something being over something else.

Under

- *Under* uses both hands. The sign will be made at about chest level.

- The stationary hand will be flat and horizontal and will face the ground.

- Create a flat palm with the dominant hand. The thumb will be pointing upward.

- Rotate the fist counterclockwise. The motion of the fist underneath the palm demonstrates how something is under something else.

To say an alternate version of *far* begin with two closed fists. The first position is both fists touching each other, indicating that something is close. The dominant hand fist will then make an outward motion away from the body and stationary fist. This demonstrates how something is far away.

Remember to use your facial expression to indicate that something is very far from you.

Near

- *Near* uses both hands. The sign will be made in the space just in front of your chest.

- Cup each hand slightly. The palms of the hands will be facing your body.

- Begin with the palms several inches apart.

- As you say the word *near*, draw the two hands closer to one another, demonstrating how they are now near one another.

Far

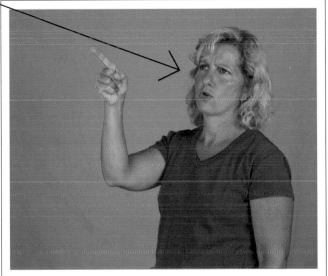

- *Far* will use your dominant hand only. Keep the other hand at rest on your side.

- Point your dominant hand and arm outward. Extend your index finger as though you are pointing at someone or something.

- The extension of the arm indicates how something is far away.

- Say or mouth the word *far* as you sign it.

WHO?

Boy or girl or man or woman, you'll have the answer you need

The four signs we will focus on here are *boy, girl, man*, and *woman*. These signs are described in depth in the photos below. Who else will you interact with or want to describe? Teachers, preachers, and librarians are all members of the community you may want to describe.

The words teacher, preacher, and librarian all share the same second part of the sign. It is a sign used to indicate a person. It is simply two flat palms, perpendicular in relation to your body. Move both hands simultaneously downward beginning at chest level to waist level.

The first part of *teacher* uses both hands. With the thumbs meeting the fingers placed at either side of your temple, bring (in a back-and-forth motion) the hands away and to the temple area again. This is the sign for teach. Now add the sign for person as described above.

Preacher begins with the sign for preach. Begin with the

Boy

- *Boy* uses only the dominant hand.

- Imagine a baseball cap on the top of your head and how the bill of the baseball cap comes off the hat.

- Close the fingers of your hand on that imaginary bill of the cap.

- Your thumb will touch the four fingers as you close your palm together.

Girl

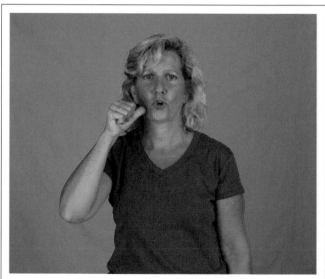

- *Girl* uses only the dominant hand.

- Form a closed fist with the thumb extended out.

- Draw the thumb to the side of your chin.

- Brush your thumb downward two times.

dominant hand forming the letter *f*. Place the letter *f* near your temple on the dominant side. So, if you are right handed you will put it near your right temple. Move the *f* in a back-and-forth motion saying preach. Next, add the sign for person as you did with teacher above.

Librarian is used making the sign for library and then the both-hands-downward straight motion to indicate a person. With your dominant hand form the letter *l* in the signing space directly in front of you. Next, move the *l* in a clockwise circle. Last, add the sign for person.

All of these signs will help you describe the person about whom you are talking. This book is about learning the basics of ASL. For a more comprehensive knowledge on ASL, take a class or see the resource guide in Chapter 20 to get more ideas of how to increase your knowledge.

Man

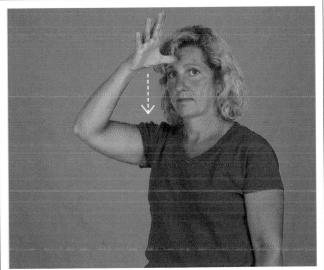

- *Man* is a two-part sign using the dominant hand.

- Part 1: Form an open finger palm. Place the thumb centered on your forehead.

- Part 2: Draw the palm in a downward motion to right

about the heart region. The hand will not change shape; it is just moving from the forehead to the chest.

- The motion should be fluid and seamless.

Woman

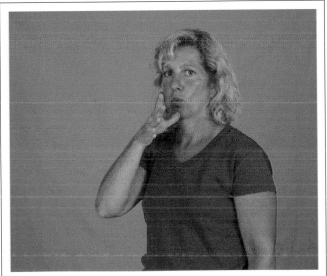

- *Woman* is a two-part sign using the dominant hand.

- Part 1: Make the sign for *girl* (thumb brushed down chin). Or, as illustrated above, make the sign for *mom* with the number *five* placed on the bottom of the chin

- Part 2: After saying girl, make the same second part you did for *man* with the open palm right above the chest.

- By incorporating the girl sign in *woman*, the sign indicates a female gender. The open palm on the chest indicates it is not a little girl but a woman.

HELLO
Saying your name is the first step in getting to know someone

You'll never get to know someone without first going through the introductions. The hellos, how are you, and name introductions mark the beginning of a journey that can lead to a friendship if you let it.

Approaching a deaf person can be an intimidating task. You're just a beginner to this foreign language. What if the person doesn't understand what you are saying? What if you botch it altogether and say something you never intended to

say? Don't be intimidated. The Deaf want to be understood and welcome conversation. Having a good grasp on the introduction basics will help you make the pleasantry plunge.

Here we will focus on four signs: *hello, my name is*. The photographs below describe in detail how to make each of these signs. When you approach a person, make sure you look approachable. Have a smile on your face and a pleasant demeanor. After a conversation say goodbye, too.

Hello

- *Hello* is a single-hand sign.

- Make a loose letter b. Face the palm away from your body.

- The palm will begin the position toward the bottom of your chin.

- Move the palm away from your face, and you've just said hello.

My

- *My* and *mine* are the same signs.

- *My* is a one-handed sign.

- Begin with your hand about 12 inches away from your chest.

- Bring your dominant hand palm to rest on your chest to indicate ownership of something.

Goodbye can be made with a simple wave bye. Or if you want to say the phrase *see you later*, start with the word see. This is formed using the letter *v* and drawing it out from your eyes (the v centered over each eye). Later is a simple sign formed with the letter *l*. Place the *l* on the stationary open palm and twist it in a downward motion.

In the phrase below you are learning *is*. In ASL this word could be omitted, and you could jump right into finger spelling your name. Yet, this seems awkward to most hearing people at first. As you transition into ASL you'll tend to use the grammar and sentence structure you are used to speaking in. As you spend more time immersed with the Deaf, you'll get used to the subtle changes in structure and word order.

Name

- *Name* uses two hands.

- Form the letter *h* with both hands. *H* uses the extension of both the index and middle fingers, keeping all other fingers closed in.

- The dominant hand *h* will rest on top of the stationary *h*.

- Move the top *h* up and down about two times. The top *h* will tap the bottom *h* about two times by moving up and down, touching and not touching.

Is

- *Is* will use one hand only.

- Using the index finger extended, bring it to your chin and draw it away one time.

- Another variation of the word *is* uses the letter *i* (pinky finger extended) instead of the index finger.

- Feel free to use either version. Compare and contrast versions whenever possible to enlarge your signing vocabulary.

NAMES

What's your name? Be able to ask and answer this question

Perhaps you've noticed that there isn't a sign language book for names. That's because in ASL people make a sign for their own name based on something in their personality, a hobby, or a physical attribute. For example, if Kara has long hair, Kara might decide to use a letter k swooping down the length of her hair. Or if John likes to fish, John might decide to use the letter j as he reels in an imaginary line. Have fun with your name sign, but don't forget to finger spell your name first.

Some ideas for a great and unique name sign are: A child who is affectionate could use the first letter of her name as she kisses it. If a person tends to act like a princess, she could use the first letter of her name while making the princess sign. If someone always smells good or enjoys perfumes or scents, she could use the first letter with the sign smell. Are you starting to get the idea? There is no right or wrong way to sign your name.

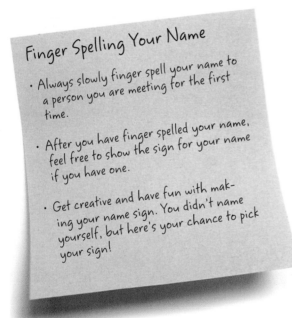

Finger Spelling Your Name

- Always slowly finger spell your name to a person you are meeting for the first time.

- After you have finger spelled your name, feel free to show the sign for your name if you have one.

- Get creative and have fun with making your name sign. You didn't name yourself, but here's your chance to pick your sign!

What?

- The index finger of your dominant hand will strike the stationary hand.

- Strike the index finger quickly against the palm.

- The stationary hand will be in a nonmoving, open-palm position.

- Your eyes and face should look somewhat confused because you don't know the answer to this question.

The next three signs together will say, *What is your name?* The person answering will finger spell his name back to you. Reading sign language takes a while for a new person. If your partner is going too fast, be sure to stop him so he can slow down. Nod your head after each letter if you understand what he is saying, indicating that he is free to move on to the next letter.

Be sure your body and facial expressions show you are asking a question!

Your

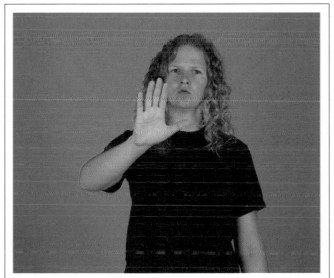

- Begin with the letter *b* sign, but with the thumb extended outward. The fingers will not have spaces between them.

- Your elbow will first be bent; as you push the palm outward your elbow will extend directly toward the person you are speaking to.

- Don't do anything with the other hand. Leave it at rest at your side.

- Say or mouth the word *your* as you make the sign.

Name

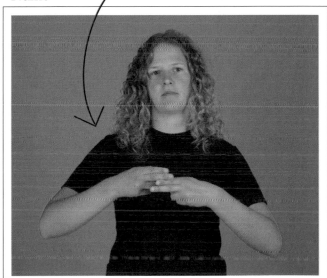

- *Name* uses two hands.

- Form the letter *h* with both hands. *H* uses the extension of both the index and middle fingers, keeping all other fingers closed in.

- The dominant hand *h* will rest on top of the stationary *h*.

- Move the top *h* up and down about two times. The top *h* will tap the bottom *h* about two times by moving up and down, touching and not touching.

51

PLEASANTRIES

Let your new friend know what a pleasure it is to meet

After you have gotten past the names, you'll want to tell the person what a pleasure it is to have met her, right? So, these next four signs—very, nice, meet—and you tell the person in ASL "It is very nice to meet you." See how every word is not signed? That is one of the hallmarks of ASL in contrast to Signed Exact English.

When the introductions are over, you may want to say "I enjoyed talking to you." *Enjoy* is made much like saying *please*

as taught in the baby chapter, but using two hands. You will place both hands on your chest. Make alternating circles on your chest with each hand. To say *talking* you will make the number *4* with your dominant hand and bring it perpendicular to your lips. Move the hand back and forth a few times. Add the words *I* at the beginning and *you* at the end, and you'll have the phrase down.

The best way to practice your new language is in interac-

Very

- *Very* uses both hands.

- Each hand will make the letter *v*. Angle the hands so the tips of each *v* are touching.

- Draw the tips slightly away from one another and then draw them together again in a rapid motion.

- If you want to use the word *very* with much intonation, exaggerate the coming apart and closing again and say it slowly. This is the equivalent of using your voice to emphasize a word.

Nice

- *Nice* uses both hands.

- Form *nice* with the hands flat and fingers together.

- The stationary hand palm is horizontal, palm upward toward the ceiling.

- The dominant hand is palm down. Slide the dominant hand over the stationary hand away from your body. Your facial expression should be pleasant.

tions with deaf people. They will gladly help you as you learn new signs. You will be able to observe and then practice how the body and face play into each sign. As with any friendship, the best gift you can give your new relationship is time and effort. Meet at a restaurant, spend the day at the park, or even just share conversation over a cup of coffee.

ZOOM

Who are the Deaf? The "Deaf community" are those people who share ASL as a common language as well as share backgrounds and educational experiences and are part of the Deaf culture. Although many people may use sign language, the Deaf community is defined through this shared life experience.

Meet

- *Meet* uses both hands.

- Each hand will form the number *1*, using the index finger extended and all other fingers closed in a fist.

- Face the hands toward each other, several inches apart.

- Draw the hands together until they touch or meet. This demonstrates the action of meeting. Because you are meeting someone for the first time, make sure you look approachable.

You

- Point your finger outward.

- Say or mouth the word *you* as you point.

- Make eye contact with the person you are speaking to.

INTRODUCTIONS

MAKING SMALL TALK

How are you today? Get to really know your new friend

In Chapter 4 you learned the word how. Now you are going to put it into practice. Now that you've met someone you'll want to know how she is doing. So, these four signs are going to form the phrase "How are you doing today?"

If you want to abbreviate this phrase to something shorter, such as, "feeling okay?" you will form the word *feel* and finger spell *o* and *k* followed by the question mark sign. Feeling and feel, which are the same, use both middle fingers. Place the

tip of the finger in the middle of the chest and brush each hand upward.

If you are in a social setting with a group of deaf people be mindful of their signing space. Be sure not to interrupt their conversation by walking in between the persons talking. When with a group of deaf and hearing people, try to have only one person speaking at the same time, or else the deaf person will miss what one person is saying. If someone

How

- *How* is a two-part sign. The first part will begin with both fists touching. The thumbs will be extended upward, while all other fingers will be in a closed fist.

- The second part of the sign involves motion. Simultaneously move each fist away from each other.

- The final position of the sign will end with the thumbs pointing in opposite directions from one another.

- Your face should be asking a question.

Are

- *Are* uses only the dominant hand. Keep the other hand and arm at rest by your side.

- Form the letter *r*, which uses the second and middle fingers, as though you were crossing your fingers. Or, alternately use an index finger, as pictured above.

- Bring the index finger to the bottom center of your chin.

- Move the index finger outward a few inches away from your chin.

is interpreting for you, be mindful that your conversation is not pointed at the interpreter but rather at the deaf person you are speaking to.

Use this sign anytime you want to indicate something in the present, such as now, today or immediately.

You

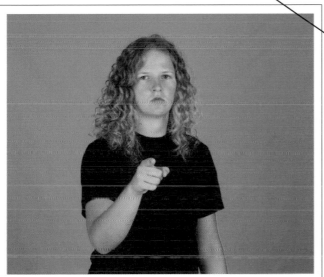

- Point your finger outward.

- Say or mouth the word *you* as you point.

- Make eye contact with the person you are speaking to.

Today

- *Today* uses both hands. *Today* is the same sign as *now*.

- Form the letter *y* with each hand. The thumb and pinky finger will be extended with the three middle fingers closed.

- Turn each *y* so that the folded fingers of each hand are facing you.

- Slightly and simultaneously move each *y* back and forth.

INTRODUCTIONS

HOW ARE YOU FEELING?

Learn the signs that allow you to get to the root of a friend's emotions

Ask the question, "How are you feeling today?" and you're probably used to getting the standard fine or well even if the whole world is falling apart. You'll find when you ask a member of the Deaf community the same question, you're more likely to get an honest answer.

Several other responses to this question might be sick, tired,

or ready, which are all easy signs to learn. To say *sick*, bring the middle finger of the dominant hand in between your eyebrows. Tap the middle finger twice and make an expression as though you feel terrible.

Tired is formed using both hands on either side of your waist. Simply place the fingertips on the waist and break the

KNACK AMERICAN SIGN LANGUAGE

I

Fine

- *I* is a one-handed sign. You can sign *I* simply by pointing to yourself with your index finger.

- Alternately, you can sign the word I by using the letter *i*. Form the letter *i*. The pinky finger will be

extended. All other fingers will be in a closed fist.

- Draw the letter *i* to the middle of your chest.

- Say or mouth the word *I* as you sign it.

- *Fine* can use one or two hands. If you are responding that you feel just fine, use only one hand. If you are feeling awesome, then use two hands.

- Form an open palm, or number *5*.

- The thumb will rest on the middle of your chest.

- Slightly wiggle the four other fingers. Your fingers should not be touching one another. The body and facial language should reflect how you feel.

56

plane of your wrist so that the hands buckle underneath, as though something collapsed from exhaustion.

Ready uses both hands forming the letter *r*. Cross one *r* over the other *r* forming an x like shape. Next, uncross both hands until both hands (still in the r position) are straight in front of you.

If you are feeling hungry, form *hungry* as shown in Chapter 8 and pair it with the word *I to* say "I am hungry." Or if you have just finished a big meal and want to say "I am full," then pair *I* with *full*.

ZOOM

Why are lights flashing? Flashing lights in a room serve many purposes. Flicking switches grabs a deaf person's attention. Other lights will flash to indicate a doorbell or telephone ringing. Baby monitoring devices also flash lights to let deaf parents know the baby needs attention. Home security alarms often use a red light to indicate that a fire is detected or that the alarm is sounding.

So-so or Average

Mirror check! If you aren't feeling great, show it. Don't smile and look happy if you feel mediocre.

- *So-so* or *average* will use one hand.

- Use an open palm, or number *5*. The palm will be flat and facing the floor.

- Move your hand back and forth. You've probably made this sign before even when you weren't trying use sign!

- Your facial expression should look like you're just so-so.

Thanks

- *Thanks* or *Thank you* will begin with one hand and finish with two.

- Part 1: Bring your dominant hand, palm facing forward, to the top of your chin. The fingertips will begin just touching the bottom of your chin.

- Part 2: Move your hand in a downward motion to rest on the open palm of the stationary hand.

- As your dominant hand hits the stationary hand, change the hand position to point *you* with the index finger extended.

HOW'S THE WEATHER?

What's in the forecast? Learn how to describe what's going on outside

Talking about the weather is a favorite small-talk topic. You'll want to be sure you can talk about the weather, too! With these signs you will be able to say, "The weather is beautiful today!" or "The weather is terrible today."

What if the forecast is calling for snow, rain, or thunder? How do you make these important signs?

Snow is a fun sign, made using both hands. Gently wiggle all five fingers in a downward motion as though snow is falling from the sky.

Rain is made similarly, but instead of the fingers gently moving, rain hits a little harder. So, use all five fingers in a bent position, fingers spread apart, and move the hands and

Weather

- *Weather* uses both hands.

- Each hand will form the letter *w*, which is the same sign as the number *6*. The thumb and pinky will touch, and the middle three fingers are extended upward.

- In a motion stemming from each elbow, move the hands slightly toward each other and then away from one another again.

- Repeat the motion two or three times.

Beautiful

- *Beautiful* is a one-handed sign.

- The dominant hand will use an open palm, fingers spaced apart.

- Keep the hand several inches from the face and

make a circle beginning at the top of the forehead.

- When the circle is complete, draw all five fingers together and pull the hand outward.

arms downward to indicate rain falling from the sky.

Thunder and *lightning* are made by indicating the lightning in the sky. Remember the letter *z*? *Lightning* is made the same way. Draw a lightning strike in the signing space in front of you. To talk about the weather tomorrow or yesterday, add these simple signs to the phrases you're practicing. If you want to say *tomorrow*, make the same sign for *girl* but twist the thumb in a downward motion. If you want to say *yesterday*, form a *y* with the thumb touching the side of your chin, lift the thumb, and place it a little farther up your face. You've just said *yesterday*.

·········· **GREEN ● LIGHT** ··············

Go back and review some of the signs you have learned and begin pairing them together to form new phrases such as "beautiful girl" or "beautiful name" and more. The more phrases you create, the more comfortable you will feel speaking your new language. When you can, practice in the mirror to ensure that your face and body are practicing with your hands.

Terrible

- *Terrible* uses both hands in a symmetrical motion.

- Both hands will be doing the same movement at the same time.

- Bring your hands up to either side of your temple and flick your fingers outward.

- Bring the thumb and middle finger together as though you might flick something with your hand. Your face should look distraught or unhappy, as though something terrible has just happened.

Today or Now

- *Today* uses both hands. *Today* is the same sign as *now*.

- Form the letter *y* with each hand. The thumb and pinky finger will be extended with the three middle fingers closed.

- Turn each *y* so that the folded fingers are facing you.

- Slightly and simultaneously move each *y* back and forth.

59

LOCATION, LOCATION, LOCATION
Be able to ask and describe where you live

Making small talk with a deaf co-worker, friend, or community member is a great way to practice your signing skills. Use this opportunity to learn more about the person and find ways to connect with her. You might begin to build a unique friendship while acquiring a new language! Location is always important, so find out where the person lives and be prepared to describe where you live. Prepare answers to these questions ahead of time so that when the time comes

to respond you'll already know the signs and won't be sign stammering. The following four signs form the phrase "Where do you live?"

Answers to this question might be the city or country. *City* is formed using both hands. The tips of each hand will touch each other as though they are forming a roof top. Twist each wrist as they touch to form roof after roof indicating a city. This sign can also be used for *town* if you just tap the tips of

Where?

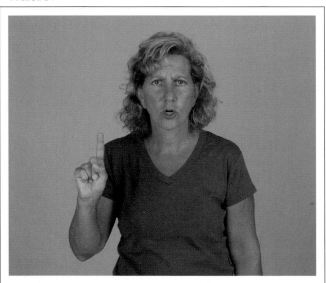

- *Where?* is a one-handed sign. You will use your dominant hand.

- Extend the index finger up, keeping all other fingers in a closed fist.

- Move your index finger back and forth by shifting your wrist to the left and then to the right several times.

- Have your question face on. Speak or mouth the word *where* as you sign.

Do

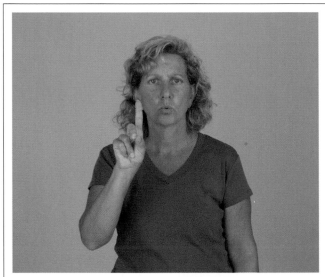

- *Do* uses only one hand.

- You will quickly finger spell this word.

- Form the letter *d* by making a circle with the thumb and middle finger while the in-

dex finger is extended. The ring finger and pinky finger are closed.

- Quickly follow the *d* with the letter *o* forming the word *do*.

the fingers together and not make alternate roof tops.

Country uses the letter y with the dominant hand. Place it on the elbow of the stationary hand and move it in a circular motion. Remember, you can always fall back on the American Manual Alphabet to finger spell your responses. Although finger spelling may take just a bit longer, you will know with certainty you will be understood.

•••••••••••••••••• RED ● LIGHT ••••••••••••••

Just as facial expression and body language help convey expression while signing, watch your body language even when it isn't your turn to sign. Crossed arms, wandering eyes, and other body language cues will make you appear disinterested and rude.

You

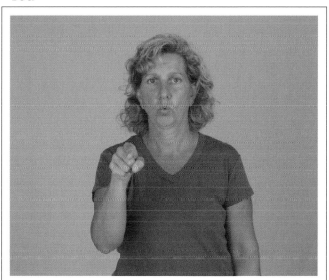

- Point your finger outward.
- Say or mouth the word *you* as you point.
- Make eye contact with the person you are speaking to.

Live

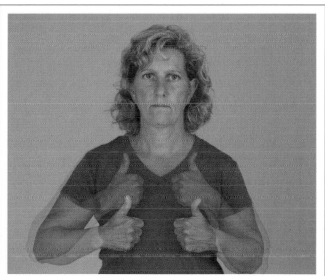

- *Live* uses both hands.
- Begin with forming two fists, thumbs of each hand extended.
- Place the fists on either side of your waist.
- In an upward motion, bring both hands to your shoulders. Your hands will remain in the same position the entire time.

AGE

Young or old, it's not about the number but about how you feel

After you get past age twenty, conversations usually avoid the sometimes touchy subject of age. But in the deaf world, age is another interesting fact that helps others learn more about you. The Deaf often divulge details in an effort to know and understand you better. If you feel shy answering the age question, have fun with it. Give a fun-but-generalized answer such as "old" or "young" or say a number obviously not your age.

Old is a sign that employs varying degrees of emphasis. If someone is describing something that is very old, he will draw his hand down farther, and his face will convey the expression of something old. Or, if he is asking, as in this context, how old you are or your child is, the expression used is not as dramatic. Look in the mirror and practice saying old with emphasis.

In ASL you could also ask this question by using the signs

How?

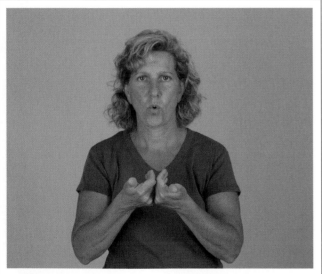

- *How* is a two-part sign. The first part will begin with both fists touching. The thumbs will be extended upward, while all other fingers are in a closed fist.

- The second part of the sign involves motion. Simultaneously move each fist away from each other.

- The final position of the sign will end with the thumbs pointing in opposite directions from one another.

- Your face should be asking a question.

Old

As you form this sign, envision that your hand is creating a beard of an old person off your chin.

- *Old* uses only one hand.

- Form the letter *o* with the dominant hand; all fingers will be closed together, fingertips resting on the thumb.

- Place the thumb side of the *o* on the bottom of your chin.

- Pull the *o* away from your chin. The older the person is, the longer you will draw the *o* down.

how old you, thus omitting the word *are*. As you get more used to speaking in ASL you will get more comfortable speaking without using every word.

Are

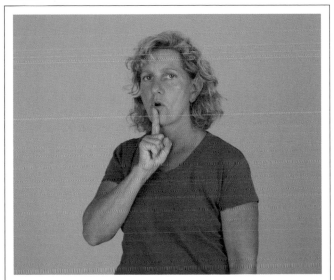

- *Are* uses only the dominant hand. Keep the other hand and arm at rest on your side.

- Form the letter *r*, which uses the second and middle fingers, as though you were crossing your fingers.

Or, simply draw the index finger to the chin, as shown above.

- Bring the *r* to the bottom center of your chin.

- Move the *r* outward a few inches away from your chin.

You

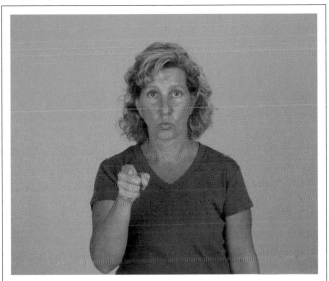

- *You* uses only one hand.

- Point your finger outward.

- Say or mouth the word *you* as you point.

- Make eye contact with the person you are speaking to. Have a questioning look while you ask.

ABOUT THE FAMILY

Focus on your friend's family to learn more

As with all people, family is a focal point for the Deaf. When engaging in these new conversations and finding yourself stumbling over signs you have not yet learned, remember to speak the words clearly. Many Deaf can use their speech-reading abilities to understand the words you may not know the signs for.

Got kids? Perhaps you have been blessed with twins. You can answer *twins* by making the letter *t* with your dominant hand and moving the *t* from one side of the chin to the other side of the chin. If you wanted to indicate the twins as identical, simply finger spell *I* then *d* before the sign *twins*. If the twins are fraternal, then you would finger spell a shortened *frat*.

If you have two girls and one boy answer with the number *2* and then the sign for *girls* and then the number *1* followed by *boy*.

Have?

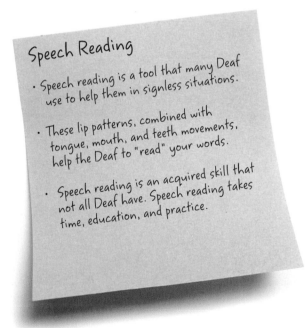

Speech Reading

- Speech reading is a tool that many Deaf use to help them in signless situations.

- These lip patterns, combined with tongue, mouth, and teeth movements, help the Deaf to "read" your words.

- Speech reading is an acquired skill that not all Deaf have. Speech reading takes time, education, and practice.

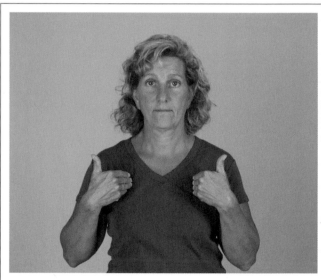

- *Have* uses both hands.

- Each hand will be in a flat palm position with the fingers together.

- Bring the tips of each hand to the front of the chest.

- Say or mouth the word *have* as you sign it. Be sure your face is asking a question.

Age is usually the question that follows after discovering how many kids one has. To say *years*, circle the dominant fist around the stationary fist. To say *months*, use both index fingers. Place the dominant index finger perpendicular to the stationary index finger. Slide the dominant finger down the stationary finger.

The following four signs will form the phrase, "Do you have any children?"

ZOOM

What is a hearing aid? A hearing aid is a device that electronically amplifies sound through a small speaker placed in the ear canal. Hearing aids do not help those who are profoundly deaf because there must be some residual hearing in order for the hearing aid to work. All sounds are amplified, including background noise (traffic, crowd chatter, etc.).

Any

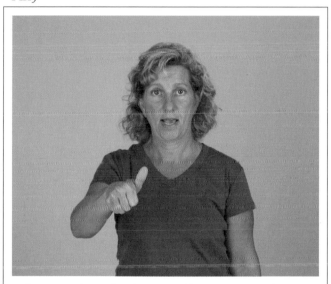

- *Any* uses only one hand.

- Form the letter *a* with your dominant hand.

- Begin with turning the thumb and fist toward your chest.

- Next, turn your wrist outward so that the motion will end with the thumb and wrist facing the opposite direction from where they started.

Children

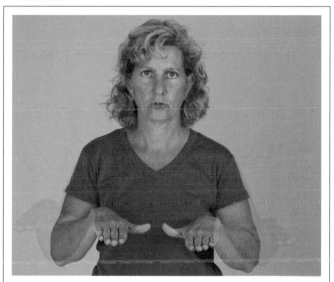

- *Children* uses both hands.

- Begin with both hands palms facing the ground about midchest level. The hands will be close together but not touching.

- Simultaneously move both hands outward in a slight arc motion.

- Say or mouth the word *children* as you sign the word.

WORK MATTERS

Do you teach? Are you in business? Be able to ask about someone's occupation

The next questions are just conversation starters for you. Think about other questions you might want to ask about the person, such as what sports does she like, is she in school, etc. Pair signs from other chapters in this book such as the sporting chapter or the education chapter to enlarge your signing conversation starters. You'll find that other than hear-

ing loss, the person may be just like you!

These next four signs will teach you the phrase "What kind of work do you do?" You'll notice that the *what* featured here is different from the one taught on page 50. Simply hold out each palm with a quizzical expression.

So, what do you do? If you work in an *office*, respond by

What?

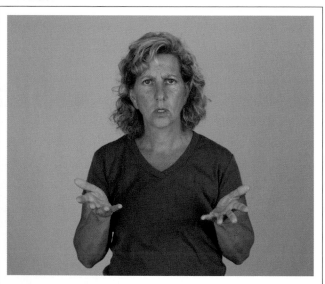

- *What* uses both hands.

- Extend both hands out, palm facing upward.

- Slightly move the hands in and away from your body several times.

- Say or mouth the word *what* as you ask the question. Double check your facial expression.

Kind

- *Kind* will use both hands.

- Begin with forming the letter *k* with each hand.

- The dominant letter *k* will circle the stationary hand.

- The sign will end with the tip of your middle finger on top of the stationary letter *k* hand.

forming an *o* with each hand. Begin with each *o* touching (fingers facing one another). Then, in an outward arc like motion, move them away from one another and then bring them back together again. If you are a stay-at-home mother, then respond with *mom*. Perhaps you have your own business or are in business. Say *business* by forming the letter *b* with your dominant hand and sweep it back and forth over the stationary hand. The stationary hand is also in a letter *b* position but is turned vertically.

Work

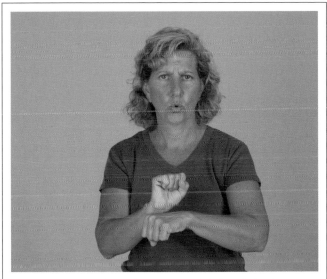

- *Work* will use both hands.

- Each hand will form a closed fist.

- The dominant fist or hand will rest on top of the stationary hand.

- Lightly knock the dominant fist on the stationary fist to say *work*.

Do

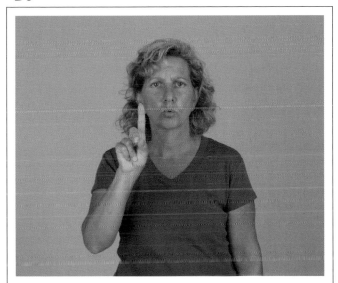

- *Do* uses only one hand.

- You will quickly finger spell this word.

- Form the letter *d* by making a circle with the thumb and middle finger while the in-dex finger is extended. The ring finger and pinky finger are closed.

- Quickly follow the *d* with the letter *o*, forming the word *do*.

DIRECTIONS
Get to where you need to be by knowing where to go and how you get there

Whether it is learning how to ask for directions for a sign, directions to the mall, or directions on filling out a form, knowing how to ask for directions is something that any beginner should know.

The next four signs will form the phrase, "I need to ask for directions." You could also take out *to ask* and *for* and simply say "I need directions." You can incorporate signs from other chapters from school, sports, and work to ask for directions specific to events.

Directions usually involve turning one direction or another. To say *turn right*, form the letter *r* with your right hand and move it outward. To say *turn left*, form the letter *l* with your

Need

- *Need* is a one-handed sign.

- Form the letter *x* with your dominant hand using your index finger. All other fingers will remain closed.

- Move your wrist in a back-and-forth motion.

- Convey a sense of need on your face.

Ask

- *Ask* uses both hands.

- Place hands palm to palm, much like a praying position, but with the tips of the fingers pointing straight ahead.

- Rotate the hands toward your body.

- The motion finishes with the hands upright, still pressed together, touching.

left hand and move it outward. If you want to describe a stop sign, use the sign *stop*. *Stop* is made using your stationary hand in a flat, fingers-together, palm-facing-upward position. The dominant hand will be a perpendicular, flat, fingers-together position, striking the stationary hand. You can always finger spell words or directions if you aren't sure how to sign.

You can either include or exclude the use of *for* in this phrase.

For

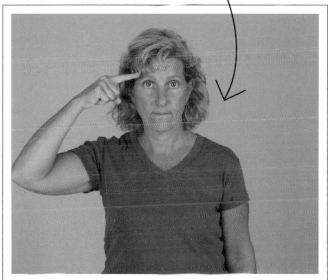

- *For* uses only one hand.

- Place the dominant index finger on your temple.

- Next, rotate the finger outward.

- The index finger will no longer be touching the temple.

Directions

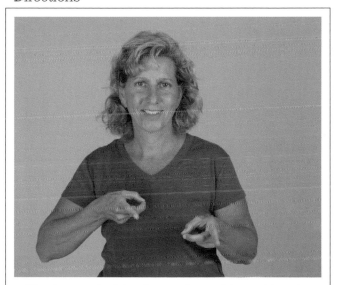

- *Directions* uses both hands.

- Form the letter *d* with each hand. The middle finger and thumb will touch, and the index finger will be extended. All other fingers are closed in.

- Lay each letter *d* down in horizontal position lined up beside one another.

- In alternating back and forth movements, move the *d* in opposite directions.

HOW'S THE WAIT?

Describe how long the wait will be, whether it's long or short, hours or minutes

Nobody likes a wait. Whether at a restaurant, at the doctor's office, at a sporting event or show, people want to know how much longer! The next four signs will help you to say, "Is the wait long or short?"

Wait time is measured in minutes and hours. To say *the wait is 15 minutes*, begin with saying the number 15. *Minutes* is

made using both hands. The stationary hand will be a flat palm perpendicular to your body. Make the number *1* with the dominant hand and press it next to the palm. Tick the finger downward about a quarter-circle in a clockwise direction to indicate the minute hand on a clock.

To say *the wait is 1 hour,* begin with saying the number *1.*

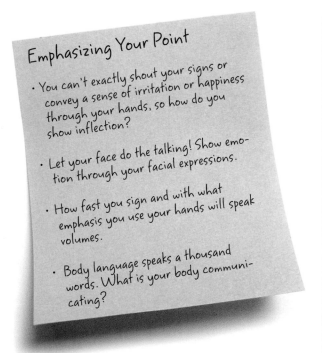

Emphasizing Your Point

- You can't exactly shout your signs or convey a sense of irritation or happiness through your hands, so how do you show inflection?

- Let your face do the talking! Show emotion through your facial expressions.

- How fast you sign and with what emphasis you use your hands will speak volumes.

- Body language speaks a thousand words. What is your body communicating?

Wait

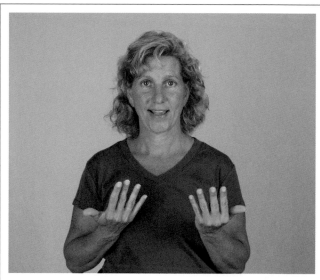

- *Wait* uses both hands.

- The hands will both be in an open-palm position, fingers spaced apart, palms facing the body.

- Slightly wiggle the fingers back and forth.

- Your facial expression should reflect a slight frustration associated with waiting.

Then you'll make the same sign for *minutes* as described above, but now make a full circle with the index finger, indicating the hour on a clock.

To say *now*, make the *today* sign. To say *later*, form the letter *l* with the dominant hand. Touch the thumb to the flat palm of the stationary hand that is perpendicular to your body. Begin with the *l* in an upright position. Rotate the *l* outward until it is horizontal or flat.

To say the *wait will be quick*, simply snap both hands simultaneously.

> ·········· GREEN ● LIGHT ··············
>
> Take advantage of the wait by learning new signs. Peruse the menu and ask your new friend to teach you the signs for various foods. Look around the restaurant for interesting words you do not yet know. Turn the wait into some learning time.

Long

To add emphasis, draw out how long it takes you to make this sign, indicating a long passing of time.

- *Long* uses both hands.

- Extend the stationary arm straight out in front of you.

- With your dominant index finger begin to trace the length of the arm.

- Move the index finger from the back of the hand all the way up your arm.

Short

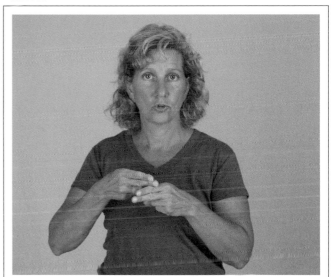

- *Short* uses both hands.

- Each hand will form the letter *h*, with the index and middle fingers extended and pressed together. All other fingers are closed.

- Similar to the sign name, the dominant *h* will rest on top of the stationary *h*.

- Slide the dominant *h* back and forth over the stationary *h*.

GRAB A BITE TO EAT
Sharing a meal with your new friend helps break the ice

Sharing a meal with a person is a great way to get to know someone better. You can not only enjoy good food but also practice your new conversation skills. Unlike the hearing, you can even talk through your hands when your mouth is completely full! Or you can relay an order across a busy restaurant without ever crossing the room.

The following four signs will teach you how to say the phrase "Let's go eat at a restaurant."

What are you hungry for? Do you have a craving for a hamburger? *Hamburger* is an easy sign. Place one palm on top of the other, kind of like you would do if you were clapping, and then alternate which hand is on top. To say *French fries*, form the letter *f* with your dominant hand. Then move the letter f outward and do the *f* again.

Feel like a bite of Mexican food? Form the letter *v* with each hand and place the *v* on either side of the mouth. Next, brush

Restaurant

- *Restaurant* uses only one hand.

- Form the letter *r* with your dominant hand. The second and middle fingers will be crossed.

- Place the letter *r* on one side of your mouth.

- In an arc motion, move the *r* to the other side of your mouth.

You and I

- *You and I* use only one hand.

- Form the letter *v* with your dominant hand.

- Move the *v* back and forth from the elbow.

- The *v* is symbolic of both the you and the I.

the *v* away from the face two times to say *Mexican*.

Or maybe you are more in the mood for Chinese food. To say *Chinese*, place the tip of your dominant pinky finger at the corner of the same side eye. Rotate the wrist back and forth.

········· YELLOW ● LIGHT ··········

Ever see a deaf couple or group in a restaurant? Be polite and don't stare at them. Staring is the equivalent of eavesdropping on their conversation. Unless you intend to walk over and begin a conversation with them, let them enjoy their privacy like any other hearing couple or group in the restaurant.

Go

- *Go* uses only one hand.

- Place the hand between your chest and chin.

- Form an open *c* shape. Move the hand to the right if using your right hand or to the left if using your left hand.

- Finish the motion by closing your fingers and thumb together.

Eat

- *Eat* uses only one hand.

- Close your fingers together so the tips meet the thumb,

- Place the tips of your fingers on your lips as though you are feeding yourself some food.

- Move the fingertips to and away from your lips a few times.

BATHROOM BREAK
You need to know where for when you got to go

Every outing usually involves two events—needing to find a restroom and eventually leaving. The use of gestures in situations like these can be very helpful. Often describing where to go involves just a few motions. To describe going straight, just point straight ahead. If something is in the back, just point behind you.

If you need to ask where the women's restroom or the men's restroom is, pair the signs for *woman* and *man* with the sign *restroom*. To instruct someone to wash her hands, see the sign on page 114.

In using the following four signs you are going to learn two very important phrases. Let's begin with "Where is the restroom?" using two signs: *restroom* and *where*.

"Ready to leave" can be used when you are ready to go to

KNACK AMERICAN SIGN LANGUAGE

Restroom

- *Restroom* uses one hand.

- Form the letter *t* with your dominant hand.

- Move the letter *t* back and forth.

- Make sure that when you are saying this sign, your face is expressing the question.

Where

- *Where* is a one-handed sign. You will use your dominant hand.

- Extend the index finger, keeping all other fingers in a closed fist.

- Move your index finger back and forth by shifting your wrist to the left and then to the right several times.

- Have your question face on. Speak or mouth the word *where* as you sign.

something or leave something. To say this phrase, you will use two signs: *ready* and *leave*. If you want to say *goodbye*, just use a simple wave.

MAKING A DATE

Your face should look like you are ready to go.

Ready

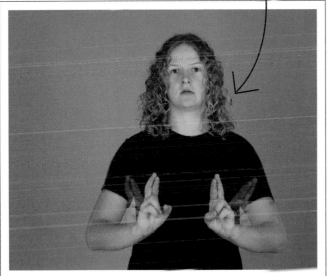

- *Ready* uses both hands.

- Each hand will form the letter *r* with the index and middle fingers crossed over one another.

- Begin with each *r* angled toward each other.

- Place the arms so that each wrist is moving outward from one another.

Leave

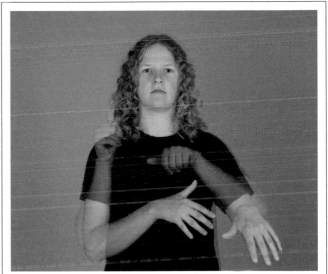

- *Leave* uses both hands.

- Each hand will form a loose letter *c*.

- One hand will be slightly higher than the other.

- Move the hands simultaneously and in the same direction toward your body. End the motion with the fingertips and the thumb closing together.

SHOP UNTIL YOU DROP
Key signs help you get the most out of your shopping trip

Shopping is a great way to spend the day with a friend or associate. There is nothing like a bargain basement deal and great clothes to bond two people. The following four signs will teach you two great phrases to use in the shopping social scene. First, "Are you ready to go shopping now?" and "What time does it open?"

This phrase will use the two signs *shopping* and *now*. If you want to add the question mark sign you learned earlier to the end of it, you can do that as well. Either way, you will be understood.

What time does it open is signed using the two signs *open* and *time*.

When you are shopping, clothes rarely seem to fit the first time you try them on. If something is too large, you can say this by just saying *big* with great expression. *Big* is formed making the letter *I* with each hand in a horizontal position.

Shopping

- *Shopping* is signed with both hands.

- The dominant hand is folded as though it is holding money. The stationary hand is an open palm.

- Begin with the folded hand lying on the stationary palm.

- Move the hand away as though you are taking money out of the wallet. This sign can also be used for the word *buy*.

Now

- *Now* uses both hands. *Now* and *today* are the same sign.

- Form the letter *y* with each hand. The thumb and pinky finger will be extended, with the three middle fingers closed.

- Turn each *y* so that the folded fingers are facing you.

- Slightly and simultaneously move each *y* back and forth.

Move each hand away from each other. If something is too small, then say *small*. *Small* uses both hands cupped toward each other. Draw the hands close together but do not touch the hands together.

To say *buy*, use the same word as described on the previous page for *shopping*.

YELLOW ● LIGHT

Is a store clerk stopping to talk to you? Remember that your deaf friend can't hear what is being said. Don't forget to include her in what is being said, even if the words seem insignificant to you. Feel free to let the store clerk know that the person you are with is deaf so the clerk won't mistake her for being unresponsive or rude.

Open

- *Open* uses both hands.

- Form the letter b with each hand. The four fingers will be extended upward, with the thumbs folded in.

- Place the hands beside each other with the palms facing away from your body.

- Move the hands apart as though they are a door that has opened. Reverse the direction of the hands to indicate doors closing, and say *close*.

Time

Envision your finger tapping an invisible watch on your wrist.

- *Time* uses both hands.

- The stationary arm is held in front of your body as though you were looking to check the time on your watch.

- The fist of the stationary arm is closed.

- With your dominant hand, use your index finger and lightly tap just below your wrist bone.

77

IT'S BEEN A WHILE
Tell a friend you are glad to see him

Let's face it: We live busy lives. Jobs, children, school, sports all fill the calendar and often interfere with how often we get to see those important to us. If it's been a while since you've seen a deaf acquaintance, you may want to convey that it's been a long time since you've seen him or even better invite him to eat or to come over for a visit. Remember that reconnecting with your deaf friend is going to take a little bit longer than it would with a hearing friend. Set aside enough

time to sufficiently catch up. Or, if you are in a hurry, explain why you have to go and try to follow up with an e-mail or text later.

Let's learn the phrase "I haven't seen you in a long time" using three signs: *long, see,* and *you.*

Next we'll learn *invite.* Consider pairing *invite* with *over* or *restaurant* or *eat* to form multiple invitational phrases.

Long

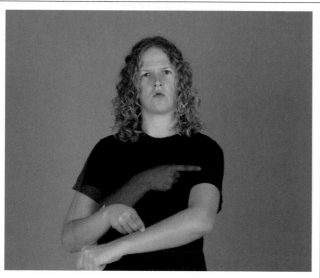

- *Long* uses both hands.

- Extend the stationary arm straight in front of you.

- With your dominant index finger begin to trace the length of the arm.

- Move the index finger from the back of the hand all the way up your arm.

See

- *See* uses only one hand.

- Form the letter *v* with your dominant hand using your index and middle finger extended and spaced apart.

- Bring the two open fingers of the *v* up to your eyes.

- Draw the *v* away from your eyes, indicating how your eyes see something.

You

- *You* uses only one hand.

- Point your finger outward.

- Say or mouth the word *you* as you point.

- Make eye contact with the person you are speaking to.

Invite

- *Invite* uses one hand.

- *Invite* is a fluid motion, beginning with the dominant hand in a curved, open-palm position.

- The palm will be facing downward, and you'll begin the sign with the hand away from your face, but at about mouth level.

- In a cupping motion, move your hand downward in an arc like manner toward your chest.

TRAFFIC, TRAFFIC
Whether there is a delay or a slowdown, learn the traffic talk basics

Weather and traffic tend to dominate everyday chatter. We've already covered weather, so now let's talk traffic. With the following four signs you will be able to say "the traffic is bad" or "the traffic is light" or "the traffic is bad due to an accident."

Running late? Say *late* using your dominant arm and hand. Bring your elbow up to shoulder level. Bend your hand down at the wrist and move back and forth.

So, if the Deaf talk with their hands and hear with their eyes,

how can they possibly drive and talk at the same time? Talking, although the conversations are not as verbose as hearing conversations, can still occur while on the road. The deaf driver can see with peripheral vision or give full attention for a moment while at a stop light or stop sign. The deaf driver can respond using one hand while one hand is on the steering wheel. If the traffic gets backed up, or if on an unknown road the deaf driver will usually postpone conversation until

Traffic

- *Traffic* is made using both hands.

- Both hands will be in an open-palm position facing downward and will be in a slightly bent position.

- One hand is placed slightly behind the other, indicating a row of traffic.

- Slightly and simultaneously move the hands back and forth to indicate a stop-and-go movement of traffic.

Bad

- *Bad* uses only one hand.

- The dominant hand will form the number *five* with four fingers extended and the thumb folded over the palm.

- To begin, place the tip of the *5* on the outside of your mouth.

- Next, turn your wrist until the palm is facing downward and away from your mouth. Remember that your face should reflect the badness of the situation.

he feels more comfortable talking while driving. Although there are more silent moments in a conversation, talking while driving is possible.

Many signs are the acting out of the actual word, such as accident.

Light

- *Light* uses both hands.

- With the fingers open, similar to a loose *5*, extend your middle fingers slightly downward with both hands.

- Face the two hands toward each other so that the two middle fingers almost touch.

- In a smooth motion, twist the wrists toward your body so that the middle fingers are now facing your face. Your face should reflect a sense of ease.

Accident

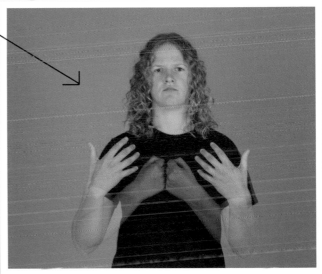

- *Accident* uses both hands.

- The sign emulates two cars crashing into each other.

- Begin with each hand at opposite sides of the body moving toward one another.

- As the hands near each other they turn into closed fists and bump into each other.

81

HOW DO I DRESS?

Know what to wear and how to dress for your date

Knowing how to dress for an event or occasion is an important factor for any social setting. Here you will learn how to say, "What should I wear? Dress-up/fancy or casual?"

When you make a date with a group of Deaf, be prepared to stay a while. Time is not as rigidly adhered to within the Deaf community as it is within the hearing community. Social gatherings tend to last many hours and may not end when you would expect them to end. If a deaf person is running late, it is often because he has gotten hung up on the telephone or delayed talking to someone.

Consider how easily you can talk on the phone as you clean, do dishes, or do laundry. When a deaf person is on the phone, whether through video conferencing (the preferred method of communication) or through a TDD (teletype for the deaf), it is the only activity he can do. Signing words and typing words take longer to do than verbally speaking, and

What?

- *What* uses both hands.

- Extend both hands out, palms facing upward.

- Slightly move the hands to and from your body several times.

- Say or mouth the word *what* as you ask the question.

Wear

- *Wear* uses both hands.

- Using the dominant hand, form the letter *u* with the index and middle fingers extended with no space between them.

- Lightly strike the *u* against the stationary palm. The palm will be facing your body.

- Move the *u* against the palm about two times.

they are time consuming—there is no multitasking. So, if a deaf friend is running late or takes a while, be understanding and gracious.

ZOOM

Does a deaf person want my help? When are you being helpful or hurtful? It's not always easy to tell when you should lend a hand in a social setting. Ask if the help is wanted. Too often decisions are made without first asking if the help is even warranted. The Deaf are capable of ordering meals, asking questions, and fending for themselves. If you're unsure if help is needed, just ask..

Fancy or Dressy

- *Fancy* uses only one hand.

- Make the number *5* with the dominant hand.

- Place the *5* in the mid-chest/heart area.

- All fingers are extended, and the thumb is touching the body. All fingers are wiggling around.

Casual

- *Casual* can be said two ways. One way is to shake your head no while saying *fancy*. Facial expression is very important.

- *Casual*, as pictured here, uses only one hand.

- Form the letter *e* with your dominant hand.

- Draw it across your lower jaw. This sign can also be used to say *every day* or in this case *clothes that you would wear every day*.

MEALTIME
Hungry? Full? Know what Baby is trying to tell you

Are you considering talking to your infant or toddler through ASL? ASL is a wonderful tool to equip babies to communicate with their parents and caregivers. Many parents don't take advantage of this tool because of myths surrounding the use of ASL for babies.

Myth 1: "Teaching my baby to sign will ultimately delay her speech development."

Many parents don't even attempt to teach ASL to their baby because they fear that the baby may become so accustomed to using ASL that it will not need to talk with words. Nothing could be further than the truth. Research proves that the frequent and consistent use of ASL with a baby will only enhance verbal development and give the baby a way to communicate to you sooner. Babies are not developmentally able to speak words at the age of six to eight months, but through their hands they can talk to you.

Value of Signing with Your Baby

- Teaching babies the simple signs is worth the time and effort.

- Signing gives babies a way to communicate to parents or caregivers when their verbal abilities aren't yet developed.

- Babies can use signs to tell their parents what they want or need.

- Research shows that the use of sign language with babies helps language acquisition, reduces frustration, and increases cognitive understanding.

Hungry

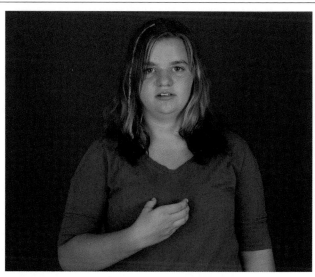

- *Hungry* is made using one hand.

- Create a *c* shape with your dominant hand.

- Place your hand at the top of your chest with the fingertips touching your chest.

- In a downward motion move your hand toward your stomach. When using the sign in ASL you will want to be sure your face looks famished.

Don't delay starting. Although it is never too late to begin, the earlier you begin, the more your baby will see the benefits. Use sign everyday as you eat, bathe, drive, and read to Baby. Any time you talk to Baby is a good time to sign to Baby. Certainly, if you choose not to sign your child won't be harmed, but why not give Baby the tools to begin talking to you as soon as possible?

A good time to introduce sign to your baby is at mealtime. Signing at mealtime can be easily integrated into the normal routine. Sign as you talk, often repeating the word and the sign. Try signing the word and then helping Baby sign the word. You'll be amazed at how quickly your baby will pick up on the sign and begin attempting to talk to you through her hands.

Full

- *Full* is made using one hand.

- The *full* sign is almost the opposite motion of hungry.

- Make a flat palm with your dominant hand and place it against your stomach.

- Move your hand upward until you reach the bottom of your chin to indicate that you are full to the top.

Finished and All Done

- *All done* and *finished* use both hands.

- Both hands will be in a number *5* position.

- Hold both hands upright on either side of your body. Wave the hands back and forth.

- This sign is great for when Baby has clearly had enough of mealtime. When the Cheerios start flying, begin to say and sign this word. Baby will soon be using this word in playtime, reading time, and mealtime.

SNACK TIME

Teach Baby how to sign words for the snacks she desires

Myth 2: "If I choose not to sign with my baby, I'm not affecting my baby's future learning skills."

Although it seems surprising that something as simple and fun as using ASL with your baby will enhance your child's educational future, it is absolutely true. Babies who use ASL are poised for greater success in the classroom later. Children who use ASL are shown to have higher I.Q. levels. Because Baby has had a method to communicate and express frustra-

tion from an earlier age, the child is typically better adjusted in a classroom setting. Further, children exposed to ASL as babies tend to read at an earlier age. Early language acquisition helps children with their reading skills later. Beyond the baby just looking cute with his new skill and giving the baby a way to communicate, teaching your child ASL helps your child have future classroom success.

Snack time is a terrific opportunity to use ASL with your

More

- *More* uses both hands. Each hand will close the tips of the fingers to the tip of the thumb.

- Bring the hands to meet and pull them apart again in a back-and-forth pattern.

- Make sure that every time you say the word *more* you

are signing it at the same time.

- Repetition is essential for quick learning. Not only does repeating help the baby learn the sign, it provides great modeling for the baby's future verbal skills.

Cookie

- *Cookie* uses both hands.

- The stationary hand will be flat, palm facing upward.

- The dominant hand will form a *c* on top of the stationary hand.

- Move the *c* back and forth as though you are using a cookie cutter.

baby. Because food is one of the highlights of a baby's day, whether the food is more milk or a bottle or a favorite zwieback cookie for a teether, your baby is open to communicating to you what she wants. Although Baby can't form these words quite yet with the lips, Baby can speak through her hands.

More is not only easy to learn but also can be used at mealtime or playtime or while reading a book or even swinging. To encourage the use of the sign, hold a few Cheerios or other snack in your hand. Ask the question, "Do you want more Cheerios?" while signing the *more* sign. Help Baby make the *more* sign while saying more, then put a few Cheerios on the tray or table. *More* will help avoid unneeded tears, and Baby will love the instant gratification she receives. Less crying for Mom and more needs being met for Baby are a win/win situation for everybody.

Bottle

- *Bottle* uses both hands.

- The stationary hand will be flat, palm facing upward.

- The dominant hand will form the letter *c* resting on its side on the stationary hand.

- In an upward motion bring the letter *c* up into the air, forming the shape of a bottle.

Milk

- *Milk* uses only one hand.

- Envision the movement of milking a cow. Your hand will look like you are milking an imaginary cow.

- Hold the dominant hand in fist position.

- Open and close the hand as though you were milking.

FRUITS

Babies go bananas for fruits so learn the signs for these snacks

Myth 3: "My baby is too young (or too old) to sign. My child won't see any benefit now."

You are never too young or too old to reap the benefits of using ASL. Although the youngest infants won't be able to mimic your motions for a while, it is never too early to begin using those signs in everyday conversation. Most babies are physically able to begin signing back to you at around six to eight months. But don't let that keep you from starting ear-

lier. Not only will you get used to saying the words and practicing your new ASL signs, but also Baby will be absorbing like a sponge all of your motions. One day you'll be surprised when she finally says the signs back to you.

If you have a toddler or an adolescent, your child can still benefit from the use of ASL. Although the child may have missed the opportunity to communicate as a baby, there are still so many great benefits to learning a foreign language.

Apple

- *Apple* uses only one hand.

- Using your dominant hand, form the letter *a*. The thumb will be beside the folded-down fingers.

- Place the thumb of the letter *a* on the side of your chin.

- Slightly turn your wrist back and forth.

Banana

- *Banana* is a fun two-handed sign.

- Before you begin, picture the motion of peeling a banana. Your hands will be mimicking that motion.

- With your stationary hand form the number *1*. With

your dominant hand pretend you are peeling back the skin from the banana.

- Babies will immediately pick up on what you are doing and soon will be saying *banana,* too.

From the practical benefits of being able to talk in a quiet setting, underwater, or with your mouth full to the benefit of being able to bridge a language barrier, ASL is worth learning. No child is too old to learn ASL.

Fruit is a healthy and delicious snack for any hungry older baby or toddler. You can pair the signs *hungry for* with any of these fruits and form a new phrase saying, "I want to eat an apple or banana." Although these signs are in the baby chapters, they are still ASL signs, so apply these words to interactions beyond baby talk.

Are you stuck in the same old snack rut? Consider some of these delicious and healthy options: Chunks of kiwi, avocado, grapefruit, or tomato; fresh blueberries; baked sweet potato fries; cooked edamame soybeans; bagel chips dipped in hummus; hard-boiled eggs; and cheese quesadilla bites.

Melon

- *Melon* uses both hands.

- Flick the dominant hand on top of a palm-facing-downward stationary hand.

- Although Baby may not be able to flick her fingers

yet, if she see and hears it enough, Baby will probably come up with her own version of the sign.

- Don't be alarmed if Baby can't sign every sign perfectly. Praise any effort.

Orange

- *Orange* (the fruit) uses only one hand.

- Make an *o* shape with your dominant hand and place it in front of your mouth.

- Contract the *o* to a closed fist and then enlarge it back to normal size as though you have just squeezed an orange.

BABY TALK

FAMILY MEMBERS
Teach Baby how to say mom, dad, and more with her hands

Myth 4: "My baby will begin talking soon enough. Why even try to sign for just a few months? It won't be worth the effort."

Although most babies begin babbling and forming words at around nine to twelve months, babies typically cannot communicate effectively until closer to eighteen months to two years. Your baby is physically and developmentally ready to begin talking to you and communicating to you what she wants at around six months. Why give up a whole year or

more of communicating with your baby? Without the tools to talk, babies revert to tantrums, crying, and grunting, frustrating both babies and parents. Using ASL gives Baby a wide range of tools to effectively tell you what he needs or wants.

Mom and Dad are Baby's entire universe. These important people provide protection, shelter, food, and comfort. Add to Baby's developing "mama" and "dada" by giving Baby signs. Every time Dad talks about where "Mommy" is, Dad can say

Mom or Mommy

- *Mom* uses one hand only.

- Make the number *5* with your dominant hand.

- Place the thumb on the chin.

- Move the hand just slightly back and forth on and off the chin.

Dad or Daddy

- *Dad* uses one hand only.

- *Dad* is very similar to *Mom* except that it is made on the forehead.

- Place the number *5* in the middle of the forehead.

- The thumb will move back and forth against the middle of the forehead.

the *mom* sign. When Daddy is about to come home from work, or if Daddy is outside cutting the grass, Mom can use the sign *dad* to talk about Daddy.

Signing helps avoid excessive pointing and grunting, directing children to have a word or sign for the meaning rather than uttering an "uh, uh" and pointing. Here we are going to learn four great family signs for a baby: *mom, dad, baby* (because babies love babies), and *cat*. We aren't learning "dog" because it is a little more complicated and involves a snap, which is a little advanced for Baby just yet.

Baby

- *Baby* uses both hands and arms.

- Cradle both arms together as though you were holding a baby.

- Rock your arms back and forth as though you were rocking a baby.

- Have a sweet expression on your face as though you were looking at a tiny baby.

Cat

- *Cat* uses only one hand.

- Make the letter *f* with your dominant hand. The index finger and thumb will be touching, while the other three fingers are extended.

- Place the *f* near the side of your mouth, where the whiskers of a cat would be.

- Pull away your hand as though the thumb and pointer finger were pressed together over a cat whisker.

MORE FAMILY SIGNS
Teach Baby signs for the important people in her life

Myth 5: "Teaching my baby ASL is too much work. I don't have enough time."

Learning ASL and teaching a baby ASL signs are two of the easiest things you can do as a parent. The signs are not difficult. As you have learned, many signs make sense and once understood are easy to remember. Even if you teach your child just a small collection of signs, your child is still able to communicate sooner and express better what she wants.

Further, taking the time to "talk" to Baby through your hands will give you and Baby bonding time. All of your interactions from story time to bedtime will bind you and Baby closer together. Teach grandparents and other important people in Baby's life the simple signs that she uses the most. They'll be amazed at how smart (and cute) Baby is!

Grandma

- *Grandma* can use one or two hands.

- If using two hands, begin with the sign for mom but add another hand on top of the first hand.

- If using one hand, wiggle the fingers back and forth.

- Notice that *mom, grandma,* and *girl* are all based on the bottom of the face.

Grandpa

- *Grandpa* can use one or two hands.

- If using two hands, begin with the sign for dad but stack the other hand on top of the first hand.

- If using one hand, wiggle the fingers back and forth.

- Notice that *dad, grandpa* and *boy* are all signed in the forehead region.

Consider using signing as you read your favorite book to your child. Rather than the child just listening, the child can see familiar things in the book and actively participate in story time with you. Pick up simple picture books and sign the words for each picture.

GREEN ● LIGHT

Tired of all the grunting and pointing? If you want Baby to begin communicating with verbal skills, encourage any effort to speak the words rather than rewarding the grunt. Model, model, model how to speak by speaking often. Pair the speaking with signs to give Baby tools to talk now while those verbal skills are developing.

Aunt

- *Aunt* uses only one hand.

- Form the letter *a* with the dominant hand. The thumb will be beside the closed fingers.

- Place the letter *a* by the cheek, as shown in the photo.

- Move the *a* slightly back and forth with a twist of your wrist.

Uncle

- *Uncle* uses only one hand.

- Form the letter *u* with the dominant hand. The index and middle fingers will be extended and close together, while the other fingers are closed.

- Place the letter u by the temple.

- Move the *u* slightly back and forth with a twist of your wrist.

WARNING SIGNS
Signs to help keep Baby safe and secure from danger

Myth 6: "I don't need to teach my baby ASL signs. If I make up my own signs, my baby will still be able to communicate."

It is true that you could make up your own signs for words and teach these signs to your child. Yet, why would you want to? You'd be spending the same amount of effort for less return. Many people who have full hearing still use ASL. People ranging from educators to police officers to doctors, nurses, and more use ASL. Why limit with whom Baby can com-

municate? If you are going to go to the time and trouble to teach your child signs, why not have them be a true foreign language? You also run the risk of creating a sign that actually means a word in ASL that could only confuse matters even more. It is highly recommended that if you decide to use signs with your child that you use ASL.

Conveying warning and protecting baby from potential dangers around the house are a crucial element to everyday

Hot

- *Hot* uses only one hand.

- Form a loose, somewhat open *c* with your dominant hand.

- Begin the sign with the loose *c* close to your mouth, fingertips toward your mouth.

- Rotate and move the *c* downward so that it ends with the fingertips facing away from your body.

Cold

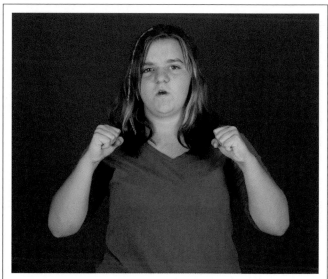

- *Cold* uses both arms and hands.

- Envision yourself freezing and shivering and the natural movement you make when you are shivering.

- Tuck your arms beside your body, fists tight and moving back and forth.

- As you say *cold,* be sure you face is saying it, too!

parenting. Use the numbers 1, 2, 3 to indicate to Baby that the warning is about to expire. Or use signs for more physical and imminent dangers. Whether you are keeping Baby from the flames of the fireplace, from a hot cup of coffee, or from getting too far ahead, Baby needs protection. Some dangerous moments can occur outside the range of a voice, and at other times you need to give a stop order in a quiet setting. Learning signs for such situations will help you communicate with your child.

Danger

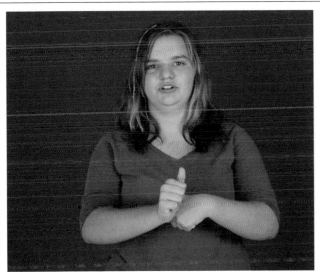

- *Danger* uses both hands.

- The stationary hand will be in a closed-fist position.

- The dominant hand will be in a fist with the thumb on top.

- Brush the dominant fist against the stationary hand several times to indicate danger.

Stop

Make the striking motion both quick and forceful while saying stop with your face.

- *Stop* uses both hands.

- The stationary hand is in a flat, palm-upward position.

- The dominant hand will be perpendicular to the stationary hand, the hand flat and fingers together.

- The dominant hand will strike the stationary hand with emphasis.

GOOD MANNERS

Even babies can practice good manners like please, thank you, and you're welcome

Reason 1 to teach your baby to sign: Signing is fun! (And Baby looks so cute, too!)

Break out the video camera and capture these precious moments. Every milestone that Baby achieves is an exciting moment. As your baby learns to sign, you'll marvel at how she progresses and at how incredibly smart her little mind

is. Baby will look so cute as she signs her new words. In fact, you'll be so proud that you'll be tempted to show her off like a little pet dog that has learned tricks. Resist the temptation to make Baby perform. Let the words be for communication, not for show.

Baby signing is a fun, active way to communicate with your

Please

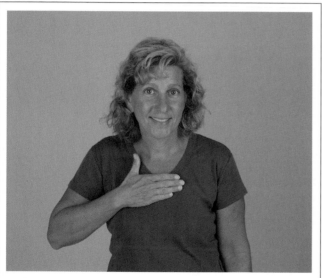

- *Please* uses one hand only.

- The dominant hand will form a flat palm.

- Place the palm of the hand on the chest over the heart.

- Move the palm around in a small circle. Encourage baby to say *please* before receiving the next coveted cookie or delicious snack.

Thank You

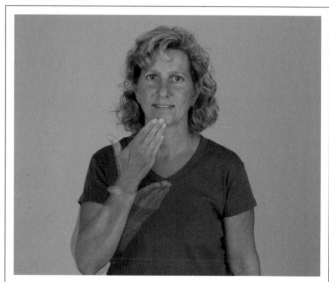

- *Thanks* or *Thank you* will begin with one hand and finish with two.

- Part 1: Bring your dominant hand, palm facing forward, to the top of your chin. The fingertips will begin just touching the bottom of your chin.

- Part 2: Move your hand in a downward motion to rest on the open palm of the stationary hand.

- As your dominant hand hits the stationary hand, change the hand position to point you with the index finger extended.

child. While you are having fun, take the opportunity to do a little practical teaching, too.

Even babies can begin to practice good manners. Although it will be a while before Baby can audibly say please and thank you, these signs help Baby learn good manners before her first birthday! At mealtime, before you hand Baby what she wants, encourage the use of please, thank you, and you're welcome. Reinforce Baby's great manners by telling Baby how nice she is being and how pleased you are with her. Your baby will beam with excitement at pleasing Mom and Dad with the use of manners.

Some signs, such as thank you, will require a little help from Mom or Dad. After you give Baby what she is asking for, help her use her hands to say thank you while you say thank you out loud. This way Baby associates the words thank you with the motion. Baby will learn that this is done after Mom or Dad gives me what I want. Model thank you in playtime, when Baby hands you a toy or is being nice.

Welcome

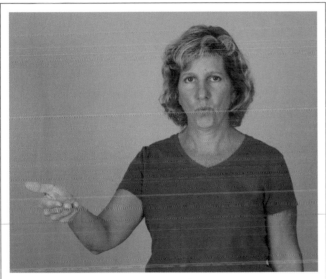

- *Welcome* uses only one hand.

- With the dominant hand, form a curved, open palm. The fingers will not be spread apart.

- The hand will begin motion a few inches away from your chin.

- Make the motion of a half-circle and move the hand until it is now palm facing up, resting at the top of your chest.

Nice

- *Nice* uses both hands.

- The dominant hand will be placed flat upon the stationary hand.

- The stationary hand will be palm facing upward, and the dominant hand will be facing downward.

- In a sliding motion away from your body, slide the top hand across the bottom hand until it is completely off.

GETTING DRESSED
Integrate dressing signs into the daily routine

Reason 2 to teach your baby to sign: Minimize tears.

Can you think of a more compelling reason to teach and learn ASL? Why put Baby and yourself through more tears than necessary? Crying and acting out often stem from frustration. Baby wants something—to have a new diaper, to eat, to be held—and doesn't know how to tell Mom or Dad. Invariably, Mom and Dad play a guessing game trying to determine what Baby wants. Sign language gives your baby

the tools to tell you exactly what she wants. If Baby can tell you immediately, there is no guessing, there is no doubt, and there are fewer tears. Sounds great, doesn't it?

Getting dressed is one of the main events of Baby's day. By teaching your baby signs, you will help reduce what can be one of the most stressful times with Baby. Reduce the dressing stress by allowing plenty of time and opportunity for verbal and sign modeling. These little moments may seem

Socks

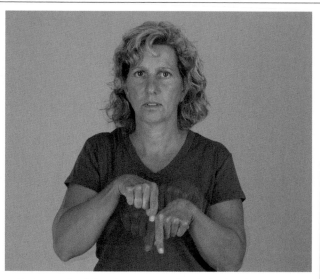

- *Socks* uses both hands.

- Each hand will extend, the index finger forming the number *1*. All other fingers will be closed.

- Brush the hands against each other in opposite directions.

- Move and brush the hands against each other several times back and forth.

Clothes

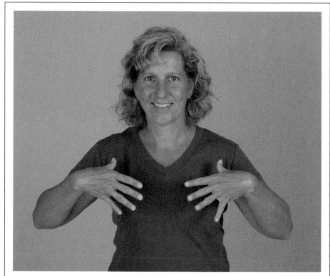

- *Clothes* uses both hands.

- Each hand will be in an open-palm position.

- Begin the motion with each hand just underneath each shoulder.

- Brush your hands back and forth several times. Before dressing time even begins, begin to talk to Baby at mealtime about what is going to happen next.

mundane, but sign by sign and word by word you are laying a rich foundation for Baby's language acquisition. Couple other words with these to ask *where* are the shoes and more. Soon you and Baby can be ASL conversationalists.

Shoes

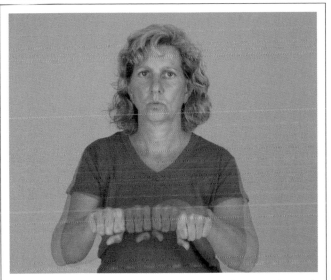

- *Shoes* uses both hands.

- Form the letter *s* with each hand. Remember that *s* uses the thumb across the fingers.

- Bring the fists together and apart again several times.

- *Shoes* is a great sign for Baby to communicate when it's time for shoes or when Baby wants the shoes off.

Dress

- *Dress* uses both hands.

- Place both hands at the top of the chest, just underneath your shoulders.

- In a downward motion move your hands simultaneously straight down toward your waist.

- Consider combining other signs with *dress* such as *pretty, beautiful, nice* and more to give your baby more signs to use.

HAVING FUN

Teach Baby signs while having fun playing and reading

Reason 3 to teach your baby to sign: It encourages creative use of Baby's body.

The more Baby begins to sign, the more Baby will attempt to talk to you through sign. Baby will learn that messages can be conveyed creatively, not simply through words or tears. Another way to encourage creative play is through song. Use finger play when singing. Babies love to sing along with their hands and voices. Rhymes or songs not only help Baby's

memorization skills but also teach important language skills such as how to anticipate what is coming next and how to predict. Baby also learns how to associate meaning with various words. Singing is also a great cuddly activity to do with Baby. Nothing is as comforting to Baby as hearing Mom's or Dad's voice.

Great songs and rhymes for baby finger play include: "Itsy Bitsy Spider," "Twinkle, Twinkle Little Star," "This Little Piggy Went

Ball

- *Ball* is made using both hands.

- Both palms will be gripping or holding an imaginary ball.

- Alternately move each hand slightly back and forth as though you are feeling the ball.

- Say ball with your hands as you tell Baby to go get the ball, throw the ball, or catch the ball. Baby will pick up the sign in no time.

Play

- *Play* uses both hands.

- Form the letter *y* with each hand. The thumb and pinky finger will be extended, and the three middle fingers will be closed.

- Twist your wrist to make the *y* move back and forth.

- Move the *y* back and forth simultaneously with both hands two to three times.

to the Market," "Jack in the Box," "Row, Row, Row Your Boat," "Old McDonald Had a Farm," "Squashing Up My Baby Bumblebee," "Ten in a Bed," "Monkeys Jumping on the Bed," "Monkeys in a Tree," "Clean-up Song," and "Heads and Shoulders."

Babies learn so much about themselves, about how the world works, and about you through play. For just a little bit each day, let the phone ring, turn the television off, and give your baby the undivided play time attention he deserves. Whether it is while singing a song, playing with a ball, or reading a book, use signs as you speak.

Book

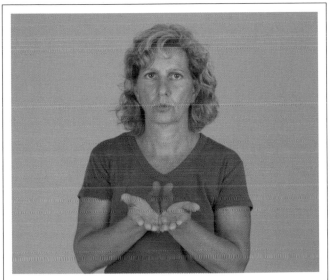

- *Book* uses both hands.

- Begin with both palms face to face touching one another.

- Open your hands while keeping the sides of each hand together mimicking an open book. Then, close the hands back together, indicating a closed book.

- Make this opening and then closing motion two times.

Read

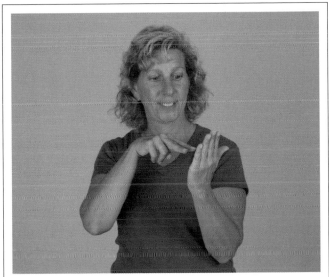

- *Read* uses both hands.

- The stationary hand will be face up, fingers together, creating a flat palm. It is indicative of a paper you are reading.

- The dominant hand will form the letter *v* with the index and middle fingers extended, but with space between them forming a visible *v*.

- Move the *v* from the top of the palm to the bottom of the palm as though your eyes had just scanned the contents of a page.

BATH TIME

After a day of play, nothing feels better than a comforting bath

Reason 4 to teach your baby to sign: If your baby has hearing loss, you'll enable him to speak and communicate.

Most babies are born hearing. Yet, between 5 and 30 babies out of every 10,000 are born with severe hearing loss. Whatever the cause may be, teaching Baby signs from the earliest months will give your baby a language to communicate with you. Fear is the primary reason why ASL is not taught to deaf children. Parents are fearful that ASL will label their child and

limit her success in life. Nothing could be further from the truth. Equipping a child with ASL does not hinder a child's future ability to speak or speech read. It only gives the child another skill set to achieve success in life.

Bath time is usually one of the last events for Baby before going to sleep at night. It is an opportunity to calm down and get a few moments of good one-on-one time with Mom or Dad. Babies like to know what is coming next, so begin to talk about

Bath

- *Bath* uses both hands.

- The hands will be closed in a letter *a* position.

- Place both fists on the top of your chest.

- Move the fists up and down as though you were scrubbing yourself.

Water

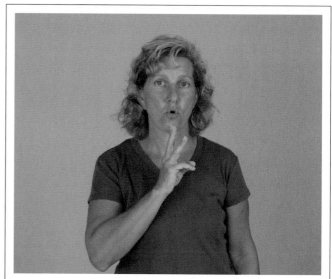

- *Water* uses only one hand.

- Form the letter *w* with the dominant hand. The thumb and pinky finger will touch, with the three middle fingers extended.

- Simply bring the *w* to the corner of your mouth.

- Use this sign not only at bath time but also at mealtime!

bath time before you ever see the bathroom. Use the following signs to talk about bath time throughout your routine.

Smell

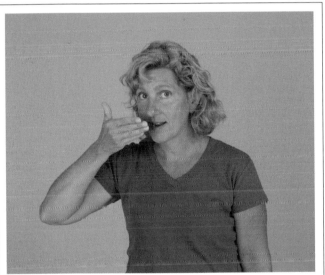

- *Smell* uses only one hand.

- The dominant hand will make a closed-finger, flat palm.

- Bring the hand toward your nose and wave it underneath your nose a time or two as though you were smelling something.

- If it is a pleasant smell, as if Baby smells good, your facial expressions should look like you smell something wonderful. However, if you are talking about a stinky smell, like a dirty diaper, then you might make a yucky face. Using facial expressions helps Baby understand beyond the words as well.

Clean

- *Clean* uses both hands.

- *Clean* is made similarly to the sign *nice*.

- The dominant hand will brush over the stationary hand two times.

- The brushing motion mimics sweeping something clean.

SWEET DREAMS

Learn signs for "night, night," "sleep tight," and most of all, "I love you"

Reason 5 to teach your baby to sign: Baby can chatter all she wants even in the quietest of places.

Doesn't it seem as if when you need Baby to be quiet the most, that is when he decides to be the loudest? Suddenly the silence of a library or the quietness of a story-time hour or the blackness of a movie theater makes your toddler talk. Thwart

those embarrassing moments with the use of sign language. Using sign language, your little one can talk all she wants without disturbing a soul. Better yet, you can talk to her, too, giving instructions that you know she understands beyond the mommy glare. After the lights are out, Baby can fall asleep practicing chatter both with her voice and with her hands.

Night, Night

- To say *night, night*, hold your stationary arm bent in front of you, as though your arm were in a sling.

- Using your dominant hand, make a broken closed palm.

- Cross the palm over the stationary forearm two times.

Nap

Feeling sleepy? Look as though you're about to drift off to sleep as you sign nap.

- Press one or both palms together and rest them underneath your ear.

- You should look as though you were laying your head onto a pillow.

Those last few cuddly moments before Baby snuggles down to sleep are a precious reprieve from a busy day. The following signs will help you give cues both before bedtime to tell what is to come and during bedtime to help set a routine.

The sign for *I love you* is a great sign that you'll use long past the baby days. It can be flashed across a crowded classroom, in a doorway at bedtime, or from the driveway as a car pulls away. Even if you're occupied on the phone talking to someone else, just flashing that sign to your child gives him a little reassurance that Mom or Dad loves him.

I Love You

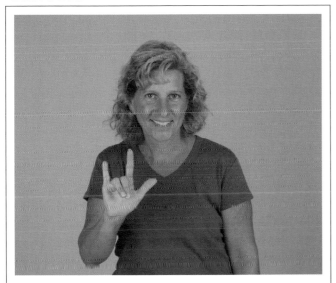

- *I love you* can be said with just one hand.

- Extend the thumb, index finger, and pinky finger.

- The third and fourth fingers will be closed.

- The palm will be facing outward.

Dreams

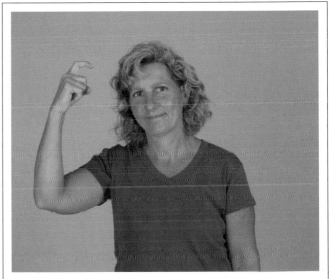

- *Dreams* is made with one hand only.

- As you wish your baby sweet dreams for the night, place your index finger several inches away from the temple.

- Wiggle the finger while moving it in an outward direction away from your head.

- Your facial expression should look as though you are dreaming.

EXPRESS YOURSELF

Teach your baby signs to communicate how he feels

Reason 6 to teach your baby to sign: Communication.

By far the most important reason to teach your child to sign is so you and Baby can communicate. Although the youngest babies won't be able to focus or understand signs before three to four months, you can still use that time to practice. By six to eight months old your baby will begin to have a good awareness of the signs and will probably begin to respond to you in sign. Soon your baby will be able to tell you

when he is hungry or full, wants to play or read, or recognizes who is in the room. A whole world of language is about to unfold.

If a baby is unable to communicate his wants or desires he will become frustrated and begins to act out through temper tantrums and tears. Not only is Baby frustrated, but the parent is too as you struggle to understand what exactly those tears mean. Tears and frustration are hard on both parents

Happy

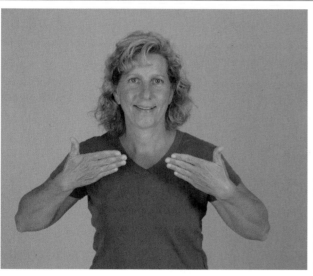

- *Happy* begins with a happy expression on your face.

- *Happy* uses both hands.

- Each hand will come to chest level, palms facing the chest.

- Brush your palms against your upper chest upward several times in a row.

Sad

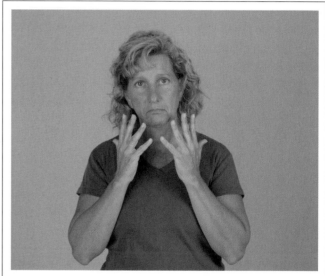

- *Sad* uses both hands.

- Draw both hands close to your face.

- Each hand should be close to the corresponding eye.

- Move the hands in a downward direction, several inches from your face as though they were tracking tears moving down your face. Be sure your face looks sad, with perhaps a good sad pucker and sad eyes.

and Baby. A crabby baby makes a crabby mom. Keep everyone happier by learning signs for expression. Remember, signing success is not going to occur overnight. Be sure to consistently use signs as you talk and play with your child. Soon, your child will be able to tell you how she is feeling through her hands.

Cry

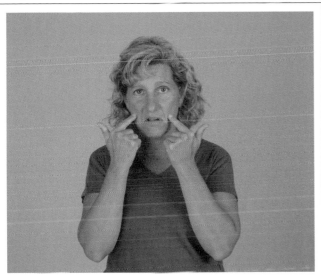

- *Cry* uses both hands.

- Using both index fingers, trace your fingers along your face from the corner of each eye downward.

- The index fingers are used to represent the tears trailing down a face.

- Your face should look as if you are about to cry.

Surprise

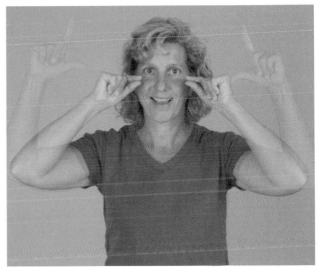

- *Surprise* uses both hands.

- In a symmetrical and simultaneous motion, press your thumb and index fingers together.

- Place hands on either side of the face near the temple.

- With a surprised facial expression, open the index finger and thumb apart, as though you have just opened a surprise.

BEYOND BABY BASICS

SCHOOL DAY
Teaching school sign language basics benefits everyone

If you interact with children who could benefit from the use of sign language in the classroom, the following basic signs will get you started. Why do children benefit from the use of sign? The answer is for many of the same reasons why babies flourish with the use of sign. Sign language is a great tool for persons who cannot respond verbally or whose verbal skills may not be as developed. Hand gestures are easier to form than words, and they give these students an ability to communicate.

Communication aids both the teacher and the child. Without communication, efforts to teach the child are useless. Communication is vital to ensure that teacher and child are sharing information.

Be sure you sign as you speak, ensuring that you are encouraging language development. To achieve more success, use the signs every day as often as you can to reinforce the new words you are teaching the child. Refer to signs in the Baby

Time

- *Time* uses both hands.

- The stationary arm is held in front of your body as though you were looking to check the time on your watch.

- The fist of the stationary arm is closed.

- With your dominant hand, use your index finger and lightly tap just below your wrist bone.

School

- *School* uses both hands.

- The stationary palm will be face up and the dominant palm face down.

- Softly clap the dominant palm on top of the stationary palm.

- Make the clapping motion twice.

Signs chapters for additional basic words that you can build upon to help your student sign and communicate better.

The next three signs will teach you how to say *time for school* or *time for lunch*. You could also begin the school day with a *ready* question. To say *ready*, form the letter *r* with both hands. Begin with each *r* angled toward each other. Then move each wrist away from one another until both hands are pointing straight.

First Part of Lunch

Use this sign by itself to say noon or 12 o'clock.

- *Lunch* is a two-part sign.

- The first part of *lunch* uses one arm and hand.

- The first part signifies *noon*, and the second part signifies *eat*.

- *Noon* is made by using your dominant arm and hand in an upright position, fingers together, open palm, thumb facing your body.

Second Part of Lunch

- The second part of *lunch*, or *eat*, is made with one hand.

- The dominant hand will be closed with the fingertips touching the thumb.

- Bring the tips of your hand to your lips as though you were feeding yourself food.

- Move the hand slightly back and forth about two times.

CLASSROOM SIGNS

SAY AGAIN

Practice repetition as a way to try to understand things better

Repetition is essential for the student to ensure understanding but also for the teacher to understand what the student is trying to communicate. If you are unsure about what your student is saying, ask the student to repeat by forming the phrase "Can you say that again?" with the two signs *say* and *again*.

Repetition with the use of sign is also vital to ensure success. Just as you didn't learn to speak English by hearing it

a time or two, constant reinforcement and modeling are required for signing success. Don't get discouraged if it takes a while before you see results. Every child is different in how he will respond to sign. Some will learn and use it quickly. Others might absorb it for a while, then surprise you with using many signs almost at once. Sign language is just one tool to help you reach kids who need tools beside a verbal language to communicate. Remember that pictures, draw-

Say

- *Say* uses one hand.

- Your dominant index finger will be extended, forming the number *1*.

- Bring the finger toward the lips, but not touching the lips.

- In a circular motion, move the finger around in a circle or two.

Again

- *Again* uses both hands.

- Bend the dominant palm against the stationary palm.

- The stationary palm will be perpendicular to your body and will be straight and tall.

- The fingers of the dominant palm will strike against the stationary palm.

ing, books, writing, song, and teaching tools can be used in conjunction with signs to help you reach a child who seems unreachable.

As much as possible try to encourage parents to continue the use of sign language at home. Constant encouragement, re-enforcement, and modeling will serve only to help the child express himself. Any effort to use sign should be praised

YELLOW ● LIGHT

Some parents of special needs children are fearful that the use of sign will delay verbal development or that these children will use signs as a crutch. These fears are unwarranted. Research proves that the use of sign will not only enable children to acquire verbal skills earlier but also give them a way to communicate outside of tears, grunts, and acting out.

Spell

- *Spell* uses one hand.

- With your dominant finger, hold your hand right in front of you.

- Wiggle the fingers as though you were quickly spelling a word.

- Say the word spell as you sign it.

Write

Act as though you are writing a note on paper.

- *Write* uses both hands.

- The stationary hand acts as the tablet of paper. It is flat and horizontal, and the palm is facing upward.

- The dominant hand looks as though it is holding a

pencil or pen with the index and thumb finger touching.

- The dominant hand will pretend to hold a pencil or pen and scribble on the stationary hand.

CLASSROOM SIGNS

CLASS WORK

Positive reinforcement and questions help both teacher and student

Affirmation and positive reinforcement give any child's self-esteem a much-needed boost. Affirmation is communicated well beyond words through looks, body language, and gestures. When communicating with a special needs child, don't be afraid to be excessive with expression and approval. All kids thrive on pleasing the teacher and parent.

As the child begins to communicate through sign, the child's self-confidence will grow. Giving the child success and the ability to communicate will help the child feel good about himself and give him a sense of accomplishment. Learning a new language deserves to be commended! Rewarding the child tangibly is a great way to tell the child "great job!" Whether it is with a sticker, a piece of candy, or a coveted spot in line, a chance to affirm should never be avoided.

Here we will learn *good work* as one way to praise. You could also just spell *w-o-w* very slowly while saying "wow!" to the

Good

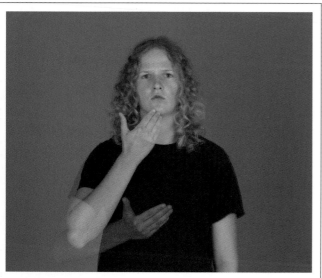

- *Good* uses one or both hands.

- The dominant hand will begin palm facing upward and horizontal at the bottom of your chin.

- The stationary hand will be horizontal, palm facing up.

- Move the dominant hand down until it rests in the stationary palm.

Work

- *Work* will use both hands.

- Each hand will form a closed fist.

- The dominant fist or hand

will rest on top of the stationary hand.

- Lightly knock the dominant fist on the stationary fist to say *work*.

child. Or say "I'm proud of you" by signing *proud* by making a fist with the dominant hand. Face the thumb toward your stomach and pull it up as though you were full of pride.

Many ways to give praise don't involve words at all. Often these subtle ways go much further than a word or two to instill confidence and approval. Clapping, smiling, or giving a pat on the back, a thumbs up for good job, or even a big jump up and down all communicate to the child that he has just done something great.

• • • • • • • • • • • • • • • RED ● LIGHT • • • • • • • • • • • • • •

If you have a child under the age of three who may have speech and language delays, motor development delay, or if you just suspect your child isn't developing like his peers, then talk to your pediatrician. Depending on the state in which you live, early intervention services can help you evelute and provide specific therapies for your child, often for free. Talk to your doctor for more information.

Not

Feel free to shake your head with a no while signing *not* to reinforce the message.

- *Not* uses one hand only.

- Form the letter *a* with your dominant hand. The thumb will be at the side of the fist.

- Place the thumb directly underneath your chin.

- Pull your thumb forward so that it now sits away from your chin.

Clear

- *Clear* is made using both hands.

- Begin with two closed fists.

- Cross one wrist on top of the other.

- Then bring each wrist apart, away from each other so they are no longer crossed. While you uncross the fists the hands will open into open palms, fingers spread.

113

CLEANUP TIME

Learns signs to help clean up, put away, and get ready for another day

Cleanup time marks a transition—the end of one activity and the beginning of a new one. Washing hands and putting away books, materials, and manipulatives are an essential part of any cleanup routine. When you teach your special needs children essential signs, you are not only giving them the gift of communication but also simultaneously helping develop fine motor coordination. The benefits of sign extend far beyond a clean classroom.

To begin cleanup time with your crew, start with a good hand washing. We will learn two signs—*hands* and *wash*—to form the phrase "wash your hands." Other words that you might find helpful at cleanup time are *dirty, clean,* and *messy.*

Hands

- *Hands* uses both hands.

- Begin with both hands, palms facing downward.

- In a circular stacking motion, move one hand slightly above the other.

- Do not touch the hands together.

Wash

Sound out of order? Sometimes in ASL the order is not the same as in spoken English.

- *Wash* uses two hands.

- Form a closed fist with each hand.

- Turn the fists so that the insides of the fists are touching.

- In a circular motion, move the fists in opposite directions against one another.

To say *dirty*, place the dominant palm underneath your chin. Wiggle the fingers back and forth.

To say *clean*, slide the dominant hand across the stationary hand.

Messy is formed using both hands. Both hands will be facing each other, slightly curved, with the fingers spread apart. In opposite directions twist the hands from the wrists. Your face will look like you are staring at a huge mess.

Put

- *Put* is made by using both hands.

- The palms are closed with the fingers touching the thumb.

- Your dominant hand will be slightly elevated above the other hand.

- Begin with both hands directly in front of you, fingertips facing away from your body. Making an arc motion upward, toward your body, act as though you were moving something from one shelf to a higher shelf.

Away

- *Away* is made using one hand.

- With your dominant hand form an open palm with the fingers slightly apart.

- In a sweeping motion, in the air move your hand away from your body.

- Your motion will mimic sweeping or brushing something away in the air.

CLASSROOM SIGNS

CLASSES

Teach and reach through the four core subjects: science, math, reading, and English

If you are a special needs teacher, you are literally teaching these kids the life skills needed to live and function in everyday life. Your work produces lifelong returns in the life of a special needs family. When you choose to integrate ASL into a special needs child's life, you are giving that child several tangible benefits. First, beyond a method of communication

you are increasing her awareness of communication and of how people interact with one another. Second, for the children who can't yet articulate a large vocabulary, you are providing a bridge to her inner self, giving her a means of expression. Last, you are setting the foundation for the understanding of what words mean and how to use them in

Science

- *Science* uses both hands.

- Form a closed fist with each hand in the letter *a* position. The thumb will be to the side of the fist.

- Each hand will move the fist in a small circular motion,

  in the opposite direction of one another.

- If the fist on the right hand is higher, the fist on the left hand will be lower.

Math

- *Math* uses both hands.

- Form the letter *m* with both hands. The thumb will be underneath the index, middle, and ring fingers.

- With the dominant hand brush the *m* against the top of the stationary *m*.

- Brush the *m* against the other hand several times.

life. What an amazing legacy you are leaving in these special people's lives.

Teachers aren't the only ones who can make a difference in these lives. If you are a neighbor, friend, acquaintance from school, or family member, don't be afraid to use ASL in your communication, too. If the child has never been exposed, begin with one sign and consistently use and speak the sign. Above all, make an effort to speak to, engage with, encourage, and occasionally extend a helping hand to these special families.

•••••••••••••• GREEN ● LIGHT ••••••••••••••
Even if you are not a primary teacher for special needs students, chances are you hit on their periphery enough to learn a few signs to engage in conversation. Exposing these children to as many language and social interaction opportunities as possible helps them hone their developmental skills. Take a moment to make a connection!

Reading

- *Reading* uses both hands.

- The stationary hand is flat as though it were a page being read.

- The dominant hand will form the letter *v* using the index and middle fingers spaced apart.

- The *v* will move side to side, going from the top of the hand to the bottom of the hand. This motion mirrors reading a page line by line.

English

- *English* uses both hands.

- The stationary hand is a closed fist.

- The dominant hand will lightly cup the stationary hand.

- Move the two hands simultaneously several times back and forth.

CLASSROOM SIGNS

HOMEWORK

Equip your special needs student to succeed in his class and homework

Homework isn't fun for any student, but special needs students tend to have more anxiety associated with homework assignments. If you are a parent of a special needs child, help your child have homework success.

Have a routine with a designated homework station: Every day at the same time set aside time specifically for home-

work. The homework should be done in the same spot so there is no confusion of what is expected when the child comes to this spot.

Be available: Don't answer the phone, turn off the television, and be accessible and ready to keep the child focused and on track. Give the child opportunity to work out questions

Deaf Parents of a Hearing Child

• How does a teacher communicate with deaf parents of a hearing child?

• It is unfair to ask the child to be the interpreter; often those words are not intended to be heard by the student.

• If you aren't confident in your signing ability, get an interpreter for the conference. The ADA requires access to an interpreter for the deaf parents.

• Consider using e-mail or writing down the key points of what needs to be communicated.

Home

• The word *homework* will be made using two words: *home* and *work*.

• *Home* is made using one hand.

• Close the fingers of the dominant palm to the thumb.

• Tap your fingertips against the side of your face about two times.

and problems on his own before stepping in to help.

Provide a homework supply bin or drawer: Have a location for the crayons, scissors, colored pencils, paper, and any other items your child might need to complete an assignment. Having the supplies immediately accessible and knowing at all times where supplies are will reduce any anxiety about not having the right materials to complete the assignment.

Constantly communicate with the teacher: Whether through the telephone, e-mail, or teacher website, be in the know of what the homework assignments are. Help your child come up with a game plan of how those completed assignments will get back to the teacher.

Any time your child completes an assignment, give verbal praise. Let her know how proud you are of her hard work in accomplishing the task before her. Homework reinforces those important skills taught during the school day. It is vital that both the teacher and the child are on the same page and understand what the homework assignment is and what is expected of them. The next three words will form the phrase, "What is the homework?" by using *home, work,* and *what.*

Work

- *Work* will use both hands.

- Each hand will form a closed fist.

- The dominant fist or hand will rest on top of the stationary hand.

- Lightly knock the dominant fist on the stationary fist to say *work*.

What?

- *What* uses both hands.

- Extend both hands out, palms facing upward.

- Slightly move the hands to and from your body several times.

- Say or mouth the word *what* as you ask the question.

GETTING HELP
How to help and communicate with a special needs child

How can you best help the special needs child in your life? Whether you are a parent, teacher, or loved one, effective communication will help each day go a little more smoothly.

Learning signs and equipping your special needs student with a language beyond sounds will help your child communicate. Visual cards of important things, places, or events in your child's life are another way your child can demonstrate what she wants.

Creating visual cards is simple and can be done with your own digital camera and printer. Begin by photographing the important item (favorite snack, favorite toy, favorite book, home, loved ones, favorite lunch item, etc.). Print the images with corresponding titles for each item. Next, laminate the cards to protect their life and usability. This simple technique can be used while you sign and speak the words as well. Although these photo cards can be tremendously helpful, knowing the signs

How

- *How* is a two-part sign. The first part will begin with both fists touching. The thumbs will be extended upward, while all other fingers are in a closed fist.

- The second part of the sign involves motion. Simultaneously move each fist away from each other.

- The final position of the sign will end with the thumbs pointing in opposite directions from one another.

- Your face should be asking a question.

Can

- Form two closed fists and place them at chest level. Thumbs will be tucked tightly to the fist.

- Move both fists downward simultaneously until you reach about waist level.

- Don't move too quickly or slowly, but at a medium speed.

- Ask a question with your expression.

aids communication when these photo cards are not available. As a teacher or parent, ensure that your instructions are simple and require attempting only one task at a time. Wait for eye contact before giving instruction to ensure that you have your child's attention and that the child is able to see and hear the sign modeling you are giving. If you are a teacher, consider recording your instructions and e-mailing the audio file or giving a copy of instructions to the parent. Not only will the parent be able to hear what is expected, but also the child will have additional reinforcement of what was taught in the classroom.

ZOOM

Diagnosing autism: Unlike other disorders, autism has no magic test or evaluation that will tell you if your child definitively has autism. Instead, diagnosis is based upon meeting criteria in three areas: social interaction, communication, and interests and behavior. If you feel that your child may exhibit symptoms of autism, discuss your concerns with your pediatrician for further evaluation.

Need

- *Need* is a one-handed sign.

- Form the letter *x* with your dominant hand using your index finger. All other fingers will remain closed.

- Move your wrist in a back-and-forth motion.

- Convey a sense of need on your face.

Help

- *Help* is a two-handed sign.

- Form the letter *a* with the dominant hand, thumb facing upward.

- With the other hand, make a flat palm, fingers pressed together. The palm will face upward.

- Place the palm underneath the dominant letter *a* and move both hands simultaneously upward. The bottom hand is helping the fist move upward.

GIVING DIRECTIONS
Signs and techniques to grab and hold attention

Everybody struggles with always paying attention, but some students find paying attention especially difficult. For those students, just sitting and listening to the teacher without interruption for five minutes are as difficult as sitting for a whole day. If you have a child itching to move, insistent on speaking or provoking other students, consider using some of these techniques:

Move the child to the front of the classroom. Keep other distracting children away from this child and minimize classroom items, students, and other children who may come between you and the child.

Give the child a friend, peer model, or shadow whose role is to consistently model good classroom behavior and while encouraging the child to behave the same. Consider allowing the child to run errands with this student to give the child an additional opportunity to stretch, move, and interact.

Look

- *Look* uses only the dominant hand.

- Form the letter *v* and bring the tips of the *v* fingertips a few inches away from either eye. The *v* will straddle the nose.

- Draw the letter *v* away from your body.

- Turn the v outward toward the direction you want the person to look when it is about 1 foot away from your chest.

Listen

- *Listen* is made using the dominant hand.

- Either using the pointer finger or cupping the dominant hand, bring the hand toward your ear.

- Look as though you were trying to hear something.

- Speak the word listen as you sign it.

Reward good classroom behavior with extra recess time. Extra recess not only gives a great incentive for good behavior but also an opportunity to blow off some steam.

Allow moments when the child can stand. Sometimes just sitting is the issue, and the child needs to have movement in order to focus again.

Don't make the directions too long and complicated. Simplify instructions and make achieving success as attainable as possible. Set the child up for success.

Reward and encourage good behavior as much as possible.

Here we will look at four signs useful in the classroom to indicate that attention is needed: *look, listen, come,* and *quiet*. All students can benefit from knowing these signs, especially in places where silence is required, such as an assembly, library, or hallway.

Look as though you were trying to make as little noise as possible, as though you were in a library.

Come

- *Come* uses the dominant hand.

- Make the number *1* and extend your arm outward away from your body.

- Bring the number *1* toward your body.

- The motion will mimic someone or something coming toward something.

Quiet

- *Quiet* uses both hands.

- Begin with both palms flat and crossed, forming an x like shape.

- The palms will be crossed just in front of your mouth.

- Draw the two palms away from one another until the palms are facing downward.

CLASSROOM DIRECTIONS
Create a classroom environment to equip students with lifelong skills

Lifelong learning, not just classroom success, is what every student should walk away from a classroom with. Giving students the tools to make good life choices goes well beyond giving passing grades. Confidence, knowing how to tackle a problem even after a failure or multiple failures and still trying again, and teaching techniques to evaluate possible solutions are all fundamental life skills. For the special needs child, having confidence and learning these skills can be especially challenging. Using some of these techniques might help guide your student to success:

Reduce negativity: It's so easy to point out an "error," a "mistake," or "something that isn't right." Those words are espe-

Sit

- *Sit* uses both hands.

- Form the letter *h* with both hands.

- Turn your hands so that the palms are facing downward.

- Beginning with the hands apart, bring the dominant hand to sit on or rest on top of the passive hand.

Clean

- *Clean* uses both hands.

- The dominant palm will rest upon the stationary palm.

- The palms will be facing each other.

- Slide the dominant palm across the surface of the passive palm as though it were wiping something clean.

cially damaging to a child who is trying so hard to do the right thing. Instead of saying the answer is wrong, consider using more positive words such as "Let's try again" or "You're getting there."

Celebrate the successes: Reading, writing, or math may be your student's weak subject. Don't zoom in on what the child isn't succeeding at, but rather on what he is. Perhaps he is a really good friend, is especially artistic, enjoys being a helper, or is good with numbers. Nothing is too small to celebrate.

Set goals and give immediate feedback: Let the child know what the goal is and give feedback along the way. When the child makes progress, be liberal with your praise.

Talk it through: If the student is able to verbally talk it through, have the child state the problem and ask what the possible solution might be and how best to attempt the solution. Allow mistakes and give opportunity for self-correction.

The next four signs will give you basic instructional signs for your classroom. Remember to speak the signs and to use them often to ensure success.

Try

- *Try* uses both hands.

- Form the letter *a* with both hands.

- Begin the sign with your hands at chest level, fingers facing toward your body.

- Rotate the wrists simultaneously outward until the fingers are facing away from your body.

Again

- *Again* uses both hands.

- The dominant hand will strike the stationary hand.

- The stationary hand will be a flat palm, fingers together.

- Create a bent palm, fingers closed together with the dominant hand. Strike the fingertips of the dominant hand against the open palm of the stationary hand.

INDOOR & OUTDOOR FUN
Take a break to play or have some fun

When it's time to take a break, you might want to play a few fun multisensory games. Enjoying games with a child is a great way to communicate through play. It is actively demonstrating and modeling what the child is supposed to do. Active play with a peer, parent, or teacher communicates ideas and concepts and, most of all, is fun!

Outside game ideas: Tape a large sheet of paper onto the side of your house or other building. Using large painter

brushes, have the child practice shapes, letters, or just random artwork. Using a large table top and shaving cream, let the child form letters or shapes or just squish the shaving cream between her fingers. Use a bubble machine or blow bubbles, allowing the child to smash the bubbles. Collect leaves and other outdoor objects. Make a collection that can later be used on indoor days for reexamination. Feel the differences of different trees. Are some tree trunks smooth, oth-

Go

- *Go* uses the dominant hand.

- Begin with the palm open, fingers spread apart.

- Pull the hand away from your body.

- Close your fingers together as you pull the hand away. The hand moving away is symbolic of something leaving or going away.

Bathroom

- *Bathroom* uses the dominant hand only.

- Form the letter *t* with the thumb placed underneath the index finger. All other fingers are in a closed fist.

- Move the *t* back and forth from the wrist.

- This is the same sign for *toilet*.

ers rough? What else is interesting to see?

Is it too cold, hot, or rainy to play outside? Here are some games for the indoors: Listen and dance to music. Create a fun box. Use a shoe box and include little knick-knacks that will grab and hold attention such as a spinner top, wind-up toys, handheld games, feathers, and squishy balls. Find a discarded large cardboard box and hang different types of string and fabrics in the box. The child will enjoy sitting inside and exploring all of the different textures. Use flavored cake icing for finger paints. It's not only fun but also edible. Bring out previously collected leaves. Trace the leaves, crunch the leaves, or watch the leaves flutter to the ground. Use a bucket and bean bags and do an old-fashioned bean-bag toss.

Here are four signs that help teacher and student communicate when a break is needed: *go, bathroom, need,* and *drink.*

Need

- *Need* is formed with the dominant hand.

- Form the letter *x* with the index finger.

- From the wrist, move the *x* in a back-and-forth motion several times.

- If using *need* in a question, be sure your face has a quizzical expression.

Drink

- *Drink* is formed with the dominant hand.

- Beginning just in front of your chest, form the letter *c*.

- The *c* will be sideways with the pinky finger toward the ground.

- Bring the *c* to your mouth as though you are taking a drink. The *c* shape mimics what it looks like: holding a glass.

FEELING SICK

Whether sick physically, or feeling emotionally hurt, use signs to help understand when something just isn't right

Many times, children fake illnesses as a way to avoid a problem at school. Bullying is a problem in schools across the country. It is responsible for school absences and stress in school and can create a climate of fear. For special needs children, the risk for being bullied may be even greater. Bullying can be anything physical from hitting to physical intimida-

tion to kicking. Or it can be verbal, such as calling someone names or leaving particular kids out of peer groups. Or, in our new cybergeneration, cyberbullying can occur when children post hurtful messages on sites or send wounding e-mails and texts.

Bullying should never be tolerated. Because children with

Feel

- *Feel* is made using the dominant hand.

- Begin with the middle finger touching your chest in the area around the heart.

- The fingers of the palm will be spread apart and open.

- Move the middle finger away from your body. Repeat the motion two times.

Sick

- *Sick* is made using both hands.

- The dominant hand will be on the forehead, and the other hand will be on the chest.

- Each hand will be making the same motion. The middle fingers will be

extended, touching either the head or chest, with the other fingers spread apart.

- As you touch your forehead or chest, slightly collapse your chest as though you feel terrible.

special needs have differences that other children readily notice, they may be targeted as an easy mark. Children who are victims of bullying are at risk for increased depression, school absenteeism, and stress-related symptoms such as changes in appetite, headaches, or low self-confidence.

If you think your child may be experiencing bullying, it is important to talk to your child, and with a special needs child, it's important you know the right signs to help him express his hurt. Find out exactly what happens, who does it, and when and where it occurs. Some children with special needs mistakenly think a bully is a new friend who, unknown to them, is making fun of them. Quiz your child about new friendships she has formed.

If your child is being bullied, talking to the teacher is imperative. Document all correspondence with the school. If your child is disabled and experiences harassment, such harassment can be illegal. See Chapter 20 to learn more about bullying.

Cold

- *Cold* uses both hands.

- Create a closed fist with both hands in the letter *s* position.

- Draw the arms and fists close to either side of your body.

- Move the forearms and fists slightly back and forth simultaneously as though you were shivering.

Hot

- *Hot* uses the dominant hand.

- Form the letter *c* and cup it just over your mouth.

- Rotate the *c* outward until the fingertips are facing away from your body.

- As you sign, express facially the meaning of hot.

PREPARING FOR EMERGENCIES

Having a plan for emergencies at school and at home

Because of natural disasters, homeland security issues, and because of disgruntled students in schools, preparedness has never been more important. We've all been seared with images in the news of what happens when proper preparation does not occur. When a special needs child is involved, preparation must go a step further. The Center for Children with Special Needs is a great resource with an exhaustive list on preparedness guidelines. Suggestions include:

What would your child require in an emergency? Consider how reliant or how impacted your child would be without electricity and water, with restricted access to pharmacy and medications, and with separation from family members.

Make a plan, whether it is an evacuation from a school or home for fire or flood. If your child needs mobility devices or has vision loss, how will he get to safety? If you are a parent, be informed about what your child's plan is for emergencies.

Practice

- *Practice* uses both hands.

- Form the letter *a* with the dominant hand.

- Form the letter *d* with the stationary hand. The arm is horizontal, and the *d* faces the ground.

- Move the letter *a* back and forth over the letter *d*.

Fire

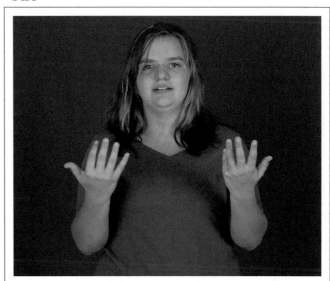

- *Fire* uses both hands.

- Face the palms toward the body at about chest level.

- Spread the fingers apart and wiggle all five fingers.

- The fingers are representative of the flames in a fire.

Consider getting your child a medical alert or identification bracelet.

Have backup. Whether it is medical prescriptions, important medical information or forms, batteries for hearing aids or other devices, or food and water, make sure you have an ample supply of what your child will need the most.

Teach your child how to reach 911 and what defines an emergency.

Create an emergency meeting place outside your home if you are unable to meet inside.

Prepare ahead of time games, activities, or a comfort item that will help calm your child in an emergency.

Create a to go kit of items that you would need at a moment's notice, complete with flashlights, batteries, blankets, food, first aid, water, medications, and more. For a complete listing of emergency preparedness for children with special needs, visit www.cshcn.org/resources/emergencypreparedness.cfm.

Here are four signs that will help communicate to your child or student important drills and places at school: *practice, fire, nurse* and *office*.

Nurse

- *Nurse* uses both hands.

- The stationary hand and forearm will be facing upward. The fist will be closed in a letter *a* position.

- Extend the second and middle fingers of the dominant hand. All other fingers will be closed in.

- Lightly tap back and forth the stationary wrist several times.

Office

- *Office* uses both hands.

- Form the letter *o* with both hands.

- The first part of the sign will begin with the dominant *o* on top of the bottom *o*.

- Move each *o* outward from the wrist until each *o* is perpendicular to your body.

FIELD DIRECTIONS
Signs to help coach and lead your team to victory

Do you have a deaf child on your team? Perhaps you've been motivated to learn ASL because you're a coach or a parent on a team with a deaf child. Other than the hearing loss, you'll find that this deaf child is probably just like every other kid on the team—excited to be there, ready to learn the game, and eager to win! Fortunately, hearing has nothing to do with determination and how well a kid can kick, throw, shoot, swim, tackle, block, or drive. This chapter will focus on basic signs to

be used on the field during practice, game time, and more. Encourage the entire team to begin signing, allowing the team members to communicate during the game or practice and fun off the field.

The first team experience can have a profound effect on the future sports involvement of a child. What kind of experience do you want the child to walk away with? The child can either gain excitement, new skills, and friendships or can feel iso-

Run

- *Run* uses both hands.

- With the dominant hand form the letter *I*.

- Hook the index finger of the other hand to the thumb of the *I* on the dominant hand.

- Move both hands forward away from your body.

Walk

- *Walk* uses both hands.

- Each palm will be facing downward.

- Move one hand in front of the other as though it were

one foot walking in front of the other.

- Make the motion several times to give the illusion of someone taking steps.

lated, misunderstood, and discouraged. As coach, you have the ability to determine what this child leaves the team with. Effective communication is the best way to ensure that the child will have a positive experience with your team.

SPORTS I

Coach, your face as much as the sign is communicating what you want. Express yourself.

Fast

Slow Down or Slow

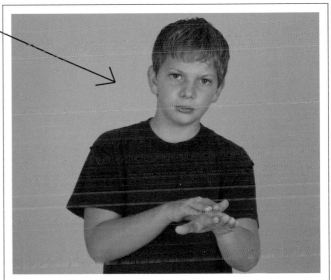

- *Fast* uses both hands.

- Each hand will make the letter *I* but in a sideways position.

- The index fingers will be pointing away from the body as though it were a gun.

- Retract the index fingers in and pull the hands toward the body in a quick motion. The motion should look fast.

- *Slow down* or *slow* uses both hands.

- The stationary hand will be face down in a number 5 position.

- The dominant hand will slowly stroke the hand.

- Begin the stroking motion at the top of the hand toward the fingertips and slowly stroke the hand toward the wrist.

COACH COMMUNICATIONS
Communicate with the parents on your team by using signs

How did you first find out about team sports in your area? Was it at a parent night at a school orientation or during a phone call with another PTA mom? Consider how much information about sports or dance or where to go for Cub Scouts and more is discussed in the Starbucks line, in a carpool, or after school. Deaf parents of hearing children are often left out of these everyday conversations and carpool chatter. As a result, unintentionally these kids of deaf adults

(KODAs) are and feel left out of peer activities. If you have a KODA in your neighborhood or school, consider reaching out and attempting to help make those families aware of the opportunities around them that they may not even know exist. Whether it is online registration, a school meeting, or a team forming, remember that these parents need your ears to help them be informed.

Coaching a KODA will mean you need to follow up with

Throw

- *Throw* uses the dominant hand.

- Begin by pretending to be holding a ball or something else in your hand.

- The hand will be in a tight fist, closed as though it were grabbing something tightly.

- Then pretend to throw the imaginary object in your hand away from your body. The motion will end with the fingers spread apart palm open, palm facing away.

Kick

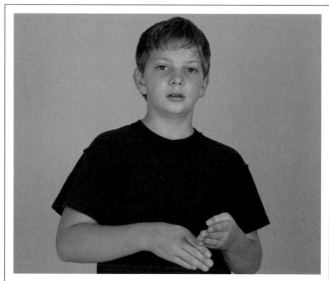

- *Kick* uses both hands.

- The dominant hand will strike the stationary hand as though it were showing the action of kicking something.

- Both hands will be flat palms, fingers together.

- Both hands will be sideways, thumbs facing upward. Move the dominant hand underneath the stationary hand until it strikes the bottom of the hand.

the parents. Don't expect the KODA to act as both the parent and child responsible for calendars, snack schedules, practice times, and more. The KODA is a kid. Use texting, e-mail, or printouts to make sure there are no questions on scheduling, practice times, location of fields, or what the player needs to have.

Swing at the Ball

- *Swing* will use both hands.

- Grip both hands around an imaginary bat.

- Act as though you were swinging at the ball with the bat.

- *Swing* the noun, as in a swing on the playground, is not made the same way. Instead, it is made using the *sit* sign with the dominant fingers bent, as though it were a chair or swing. Move both hands back and forth in a rocking motion.

Catch

- *Catch* uses both hands.

- Begin, as pictured, with both hands open as though you were ready to catch the ball.

- Then close your hands together, crossing the wrists.

- The motion will mimic the act of catching and holding something in your hand.

COACHING THE PLAYERS
It takes the whole team to win a game

Inclusion. It's a word you'll hear a lot if you begin to spend any time researching special needs education. As an education buzzword, it relates to an educational environment that is receptive and completely adapted to teaching all types of students. For you as a coach, *inclusion* means including and coaching everyone. Beyond the child who may have hearing loss, there are bound to be other kids who are different, too—perhaps shorter, perhaps faster, perhaps better at throwing

or defending. The team is a collection of differences between height, ability, hearing, or speed.

Coaching a child with hearing loss will take a little more sensitivity on your part to ensure that the child understands what is going on. Demonstrate as much as possible what is expected. When speaking to your team, be sure you are signing as much as possible. Pair kids together for skills and technique training so the child gets to know and understand

Stop

- *Stop* uses both hands.

- The stationary hand is in a flat, palm-upward position.

- The dominant hand will be perpendicular to the

stationary hand, the hand flat and fingers together.

- The dominant hand will strike the stationary hand with emphasis.

Go

- *Go* uses both hands.

- This is a variation of the sign for *go*. This variation is more appropriate to use in a sports environment where you are directing a person where to go.

- Form the number *1* with both hands.

- Move the hands forward and point each finger of each hand in the direction you want the person to go.

each player on the team. Use body language, gestures, and hand signals as much as possible to reinforce any verbal communication. If possible, find someone who is willing to interpret during games and practices. As coach, you'll also need to have heightened awareness to what the kids are saying at all times. Kids are incredible at imitating what they see. Encourage the parents to be inclusive and to model positive words. Negativity should never be tolerated.

As coach, not only are you equipping these kids with the benefits of team sports (lifelong interest in healthy activity, how to be on a team, importance of working together, and fun physical activity), but also you're giving them the opportunity to relate to and understand the hearing-impaired world. Way to go, Coach!

Get Ready

- *Get ready* uses both hands.

- Form the letter *r* with each hand.

- Begin with both forearms crossed, forming a large x shape with your arms.

- Move both hands away from one another until they are vertical as pictured above.

Do Over

- *Do over*, *repeat*, and *again* can all be said with this sign.

- The dominant hand will strike the stationary hand.

- The stationary hand will be a flat palm, fingers together.

- Create a bent palm, fingers closed together with the dominant hand. Strike the fingertips of the hand against the open palm.

PRACTICE & GAMES
Get ready for game time by knowing your signs

Preparing a team for success involves practice—lots and lots of practice. Consistent, efficient, and regular practice will determine the success of your team. Practicing with a deaf child will not affect how you practice with your team. But, at the same time, the deaf child will benefit more from consistent practicing.

If at all possible, keep practices at the same time and location each week to minimize verbal changes having to be

communicated to the child. Do the same drills and build and expand on those drills at practice. The child will know what to expect and won't be wasting precious practice time trying to figure out the instructions to a new drill each week. Demonstrate the drill and have the child repeat so that you know the child has understood the drill. Use body language and gestures when you don't know the sign.

Refer to the baby signs and classroom signs chapters to

Next

This movement signifies something being next to something else.

- *Next* uses both hands.

- Begin with both hands making a broken palm.

- The dominant palm will be closer to your body behind the passive palm.

- Next, keeping the passive hand still, move the dominant hand over the passive until it is now in front of the passive hand.

Game

- *Game* uses both hands.

- Both hands are mirror images of one another, with the closed fist and thumb extended outward.

- Bring the fists together back and forth two or three times.

- A quick way to signify if a game was won or lost is to do the thumbs-up or thumbs-down sign.

help build your signing vocabulary. And finally, e-mail or print out everything that was discussed at practice to ensure that parents and all athletes are on the same page. Ensure that you allow enough time in practice for the extra time it may take to sign and communicate.

Here you will learn four signs to assist game and practice day communication: *next*, *game*, *practice*, and *here*.

Practice

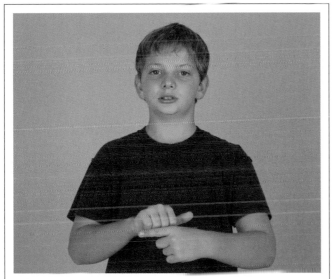

- *Practice* uses both hands.

- Form the letter *a* with the dominant hand.

- Form a sideways number *1* with the stationary hand.

- Slide the *a* back and forth over the passive hand several times.

Here

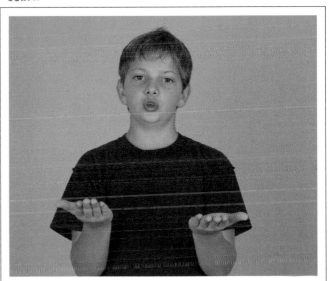

- *Here* uses both hands.

- Both hands will be palm up, flat, and horizontal.

- Move both hands simultaneously side to side.

- The movement should not be large, just a small side-to-side motion several times.

GOOD SPORTSMANSHIP
Win or lose, what matters is how you play the game

Attitude sets the temperature for your team. We've all seen the negative effects of attitude: the angry, upset parent verbally assaulting referees or players. Life literally is stolen from them. The words are like arrows delivered by the tongue. As coach, you are responsible for setting the attitude for the team. How you encourage, what you see possible for your team and your players, and what you inspire these kids to be will be determined by your attitude.

Attitude is contagious. Your positive attitude can be a light to others who may not be able to see the goal but who are momentarily caught up in their own self-doubt. With a positive attitude, you can be their eyes to see the goal, their hope in uncertain times. People are encouraged by it. And in being so, they are encouraging and inspiring to those who look to them. Best of all, unlike the challenges and obstacles before us, our attitude is always completely under our control.

Hooray or Celebrate

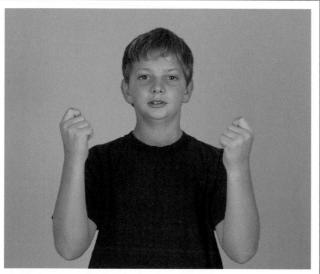

- *Hooray* or *celebrate* uses both hands.

- Both hands will form the letter *a* and be about shoulder level.

- In a circular motion from the wrist, move each *a* in

several circles simultaneously.

- Your expression should be excited and celebratory.

Fun

- *Fun* uses both hands.

- Form the letter *h* with both hands.

- The dominant fingertips will begin at the side of the nose and move downward

until the dominant hand in the *h* position rests on top of the passive hand.

- The passive *h* will face down and still.

Charles Swindoll, best-selling author and theologian, said, "The remarkable thing is we have a choice every day regarding the attitude we will embrace for the day. We cannot change our past . . . we cannot change the fact that people will act in a certain way. We cannot change the inevitable. The only thing we can do is play on the one string we have, and that is our attitude . . . I am convinced that life is 10% what happens to me and 90% how I react to it. And so it is with you . . . we are in charge of our attitudes." What will your attitude be?

Good

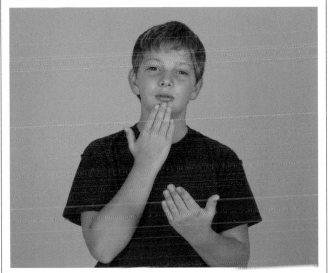

- Good uses both hands.

- The dominant hand will begin palm facing upward and horizontal at the bottom of your chin.

- The stationary hand will be horizontal, palm facing up.

- Move the dominant hand down until it rests in the stationary palm.

Attitude

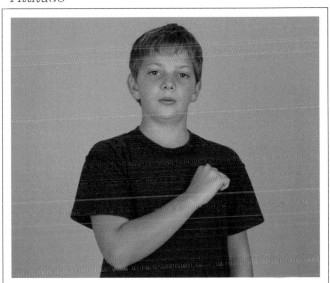

- Attitude uses the dominant hand.

- Form the letter a with the dominant hand.

- Circle the a from the wrist one time just inches away from your shoulder.

- After you make one circle, then rest the a on the shoulder.

WINNING & LOSING
Celebrate your team's successes with everyone

Getting through any sporting season isn't an easy task. You may have had your share of cold or hot weather. Perhaps you've had to tone down an enthusiastic parent or two, and sacrifice a few hours of Saturday morning sleep. The rewards of coaching have surely outweighed all of these minor inconveniences. At the end of the season you've seen a group of kids become a team. Kids have learned new skills and acquired new friendships. And for a season, you as coach have

had the privilege of shaping these young lives and attitudes. In the middle of all that great athleticism and teamwork you've introduced the kids to and have learned a new language. No better way to end a great season than with a good celebration.

Celebrations for deaf people surrounded by hearing people can be a little rough. It's not uncommon for chatter to be exploding all around them. The deaf people see the laughter,

Win

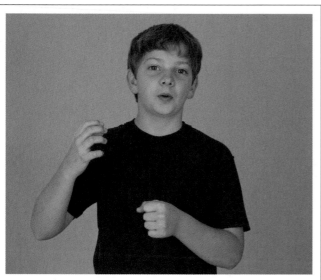

- *Win* uses both hands.

- Begin by forming a sideways letter s with the stationary hand. This hand and arm will remain still.

- The dominant hand will sweep over the stationary

hand as though it were taking something.

- The dominant hand begins in an open-palm position, but as it brushes over the stationary hand it closes into a fist.

Lose or Lost

- *Lose* uses both hands. *Lose* and *lost* are the same sign.

- Form the letter v with your dominant hand.

- The passive hand will be flat and still, palm facing upward.

- Strike the v against the passive hand. The sign ends with the v on top of the passive hand.

the smiles, the quick comebacks and wonder, "What was just said?" They tap; they look quizzically and very often get ignored, at least temporarily. After someone finally gets around to telling them what was just said the humor has passed, or it is a condensed version of the story. Or worse, they hear the dreaded "It wasn't important."

At your team celebration make a team effort to include the deaf person. Explain to the kids how important it is to let the child know what is going on, how it hurts to be left out. Encourage the team members to sign with the child. Praise the kids for being such good friends to everybody. Including everybody in the team celebration makes it truly a team celebration.

During any season there will be wins and losses and hopefully a championship game. These next three signs, *win, lose*, and *championship* are signs for any season

Championship: Part 1

- *Championship* uses both hands.

- The dominant hand will form the letter *c*.

- The dominant hand will begin at about head level.

- The stationary hand will form the number *1*.

Championship: Part 2

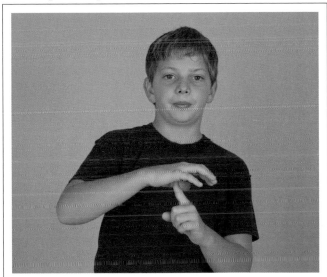

- Move the dominant letter *c* downward.

- The dominant hand will rest on top of the stationary number *1*.

- To say *team* in conjunction with this sign, both hands will form the letter *t* with thumbs touching one another. Then make a circular motion until both pinky fingers are touching one another.

SOCCER SIGNS

Learn proper coaching, communication, and preparation for game day

Soccer—or football, as it is known in the rest of the world—is the most popular team sport in the world. More people watch and play soccer than any other sport. Soccer is great aerobic exercise. It helps children learn the power of cooperation through passing and working as a team. Unlike in other sports, kids of all sizes can excel on the soccer field. Unlike in most other team sports, the goalie is the only person whose performance can singly be scrutinized, making soccer a great introduction to team sports. It is a great team sport and fun and can be played your whole life.

As a coach, you've already discovered there's a lot more to being coach than just showing up to practice and kicking

Soccer

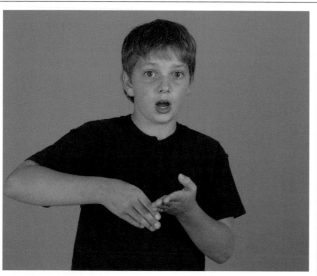

- *Soccer* is made the same way as saying kick, but mouth or say soccer as you sign.

- The dominant hand will strike the stationary hand as though it were showing the action of kicking something.

- Both hands will be flat palms, fingers together.

- Both hands will be sideways, thumbs facing upward. Move the dominant hand underneath the stationary hand until it strikes the bottom of the hand.

Goal

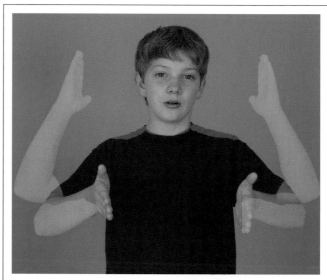

- *Goal* is made using both hands.

- Simply form a goal post with your arms, both arms extended on either side of your chest.

- To say *score* in soccer, flick the dominant middle finger

- across the open upward-facing palm of the passive hand.

- In *score* the flicking of the finger represents the kicking of a ball.

the ball around. One of the most important ingredients of a good soccer team is the ability to communicate on the field. Whether it is to pass, to move forward, to block, and to let the player know there is room to turn, talking on the field helps the team be better. Here you will learn easy signs that the players can use on the field and that you can use in practice to help them communicate better.

Proper preparation, coupled with your attitude, is the best training you will give your team. Using your new signs and great attitude, you're sure to have a season of success!

Move

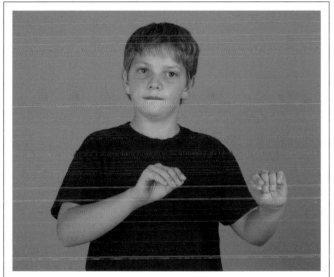

- *Move* uses both hands.

- Begin with both hands closed. The fingertips will touch the thumb, resembling a flat letter *o*.

- Move both hands simultaneously either to the right or to the left in an arc like motion.

- The sign represents the action of something moving.

Forward

- *Forward*, as shown, uses one hand.

- Form the letter *f* with the dominant hand.

- Move the letter *f* forward.

- An alternate version of the sign uses both palms, bent. Move both palms simultaneously forward away from your body.

FOOTBALL SIGNS

Inspiration from former Denver Bronco Kenny Walker

Football is a sport in which most players rely on their ears to understand what is going on in the game. Listening to the quarterback in a huddle, knowing the calls, and understanding chalkboard talks all require hearing, right? An NFL player would need every sense and skill—hearing, sight, speed, and agility. Can someone even consider playing in the NFL without those senses and skills? Kenny Walker did.

Kenny Walker is an amazing inspiration to deaf children across the country. At the age of two Kenny Walker became deaf from meningitis. Yet, being deaf did not stop Kenny from realizing his potential. Kenny Walker is living proof that the Deaf are capable of achieving the highest dreams, even playing in the NFL.

Despite being profoundly deaf, Kenny Walker achieved impressive football success. In college Kenny was named an All American on the University of Nebraska Cornhuskers. In 1990

Football

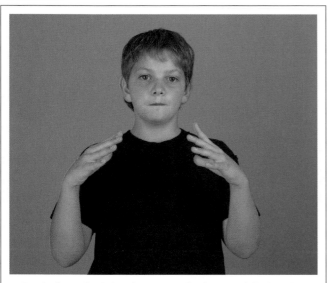

- *Football* uses both hands.

- Begin with the hands apart, as pictured, fingers apart.

- Bring the two hands together.

- The fingers of the hands will intertwine. The sign ends with the hands joined together.

Block

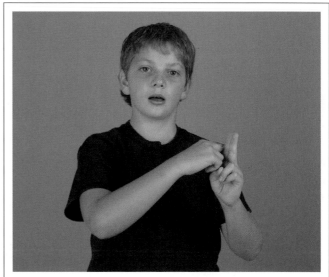

- *Block* uses both hands.

- Form the letter *u* with the stationary hand.

- Form the letter *h* with the dominant hand.

- Strike the *h* against the *u* as though the passive hand were blocking the dominant hand.

Kenny Walker was named the Big Eight Defensive Player of the Year. Kenny Walker was selected by the Denver Broncos in the 1991 NFL draft. After playing two seasons with the Denver Broncos, Kenny was cut from the team. He then joined the Canadian Football League in 1994 and played for the Calgary Stampeders. After playing with the Stampeders for two seasons Kenny retired from football. Kenny took a coaching position with the Iowa School for the Deaf in Council Bluffs, Iowa.

After his football career, Kenny became an author, publishing his autobiography, *Roar of Silence: The Kenny Walker Story*, in 1999, co-authored with Bob Schaller. Kenny's story continues to inspire, encourage, and give hope. He is a living testimony that success is not defined by what you don't have but rather by what you do with what you have.

Here you will learn four football basics: *football, block, tackle* and *touchdown*. Combine these signs with signs learned in the Sports I chapter to have a wide football vocabulary.

Tackle

- *Tackle* uses both hands.

- With the passive hand make an upside-down *u*.

- With the dominant hand begin with the hand open and move it toward the passive hand.

- The dominant hand will look as though it were grabbing the passive hand and close into a fist. This resembles the act of tackling somebody.

Touchdown

- *Touchdown* uses both hands.

- *Touchdown* is made the same way as *goal*.

- Frame either side of the face with the forearms. The palms will be facing each other.

- The motion mimics the shape of a goal post on a football field. It is the same as the referee sign for touchdown.

BASEBALL SIGNS

Going to a ball game? Baseball signs and safety basics will ensure a fun day

Attending a major or minor league ball game is a great way to pique a child's interest in a sport. Whether it is hockey, baseball, football, soccer, or basketball, the excitement of a game is contagious. Maybe it's the excitement in the air, but the peanuts just taste better, the popcorn is crunchier, and the nachos are never more delicious than at a ball game. Be-

fore you head out to a game with any kids, being safe will help make sure your game day fun is not ruined.

Before the big game, talk about where you will be going and crowd size. Explain the importance of staying together and using the restroom in groups of two or more. If the child does get lost, teach her to go to a police officer or security

Low

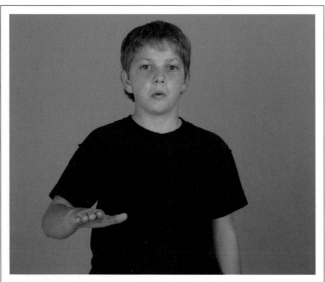

- *Low* uses the dominant hand only.

- Face the palm down in a number *5* position.

- Slightly move the hand lower, to indicate that something is low.

- Say or mouth the word with emphasis as you sign it.

Watch or Look

Be emphatic with your eyes! Show the importance of watching something.

- *Watch* or *look* uses the dominant hand.

- Form the letter *v* and bring the tips of the *v* fingertips a few inches away from either eye. The *v* will straddle the nose.

- Draw the letter *v* away from your body.

- Turn the *v* outward toward the direction you want the person to look when it is about 1 foot away from your chest.

guard at the venue. After you arrive at the big event, designate a meeting spot in case someone is separated. If you are taking a deaf child, this is especially important because the child won't be able to hear messages spoken over the intercom, so be sure you have a plan of where to go ahead of time. If your phone has a camera function, take a snapshot of the kids before you go in. In case something were to happen, you have a picture immediately available to show what the child is wearing and what the child looks like. Make sure the child has on his person your contact information so that you

can be reached if the child is found. Just covering the safety basics will help ensure that game day is about the game!

Here you will learn four baseball basics: *low, look* or *watch, level* and *step*. These four signs are will help coach baseball or discuss a game.

Level

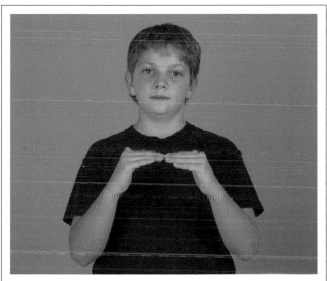

- *Level* uses both hands.

- Bend each palm and keep the fingers together.

- Touch the tips of the fingertips to each other.

- The hands should be level. If you want to indicate that something is not level, first say *level* as shown, then move one hand slightly above or below.

Step

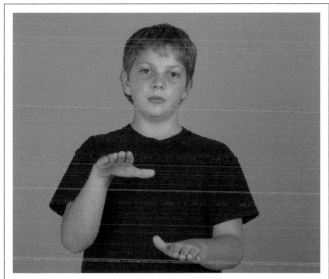

- *Step* uses both hands.

- Begin with both hands near one another, one slightly in front of the other.

- The palms will be facing downward, flat and fingers together.

- Move the dominant hand in front of the passive hand as though it had just taken a step.

HOCKEY SIGNS

Who's going to win the cup? Socialize at the big game

Whether it is the Super Bowl, the Stanley Cup playoffs, or the World Series, watching a game together is fun. Celebrate your favorite team by watching the game at your house. Watching the big game together is a great opportunity to share food and fun. These celebrations are fun for the deaf, too, because unlike other hearing social settings where the primary interactions are conversations, here the big event is the game. With closed captioning the deaf person won't miss a beat, and you'll all enjoy watching the game. So break open that bag of chips, pop some popcorn, and have fun watching the game together.

Talking sports is a great way to connect with a deaf child or adult. Sports serve as a great common denominator for any group of people. Not only are sports fun to play with each other generally, but also everybody has a favorite team and enjoys watching a game. To easily and quickly in-

Hockey

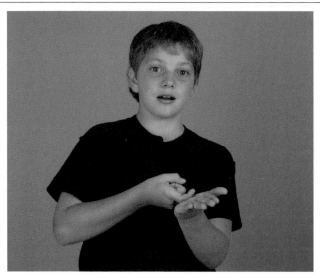

- *Hockey* uses both hands.

- The passive hand is flat, palm facing upward.

- Make the letter *x* with the dominant hand.

- Strike the *x* several times on the palm of the passive hand, much like a hockey stick strikes the ground or ice.

Penalty

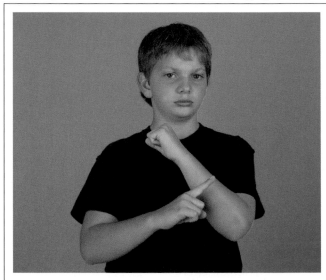

- *Penalty* uses both hands.

- With the stationary hand make a fist and place it just below the chin.

- Form the number *1* with the dominant hand.

- Brush the *1* against the forearm of the passive arm about two times.

dicate whether your team is winning or losing, simply use the thumbs-up or thumbs-down sign. Winning is thumbs up, and losing is thumbs down. Learning these simple signs, even if you aren't coaching or will never play the sport, will help you have sports conversations with a deaf person. Ask the person to teach you the signs for the names of various sports teams and cities.

The football huddle was created in 1894 by deaf quarterback Paul Hubbard. Hubbard, who played for Gallaudet University, was concerned that other teams were "hearing" his plays by reading the signs. To keep plays from being intercepted, he formed the "huddle," a formation of bodies that kept his signs hidden from other players. Today the huddle is an integral part of football.

Stick

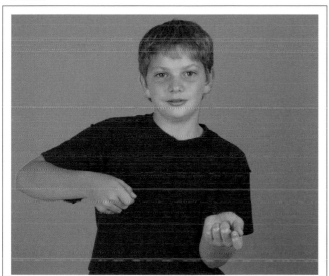

- *Stick* uses both hands.

- With both hands pretend to grasp a hockey stick.

- Your body should look like it is ready to play hockey.

- Rotate the stick around to indicate the motion of hockey.

Pass

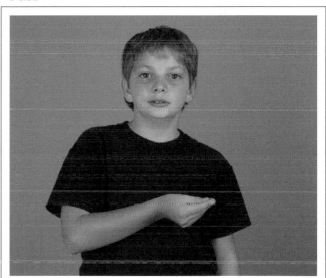

- *Pass* uses the dominant hand.

- Bring the fingertips to meet the thumb. The palm is facing upward.

- Move the hand outward away from your body.

- The motion looks as though you were passing something.

SWIMMING SIGNS
Encourage healthy activities among your deaf friends

Swimming is a lifelong individual or team sport that not only is a great cardio workout for your body but also can be a relaxing and cool respite from a hot day.

Using ASL is great in the water. Despite splashing, lifeguard whistles, and the crowd chatter, ASL can easily be used both under the water and across a crowded pool. Deaf swimmers can easily compete with hearing swimmers in this sporting environment, which can easily substitute flags and hand signals for whistles and horns. Competitive swimmers focus on four major strokes: freestyle, butterfly, breaststroke, and backstroke. Here you will learn four signs: *swimming, breathe, hands,* and *glide*. These are key signs for recreational or competitive swimming.

Swimmers develop great life skills, learning how to participate in sports, managing their time, and setting goals. Swimming is a great sport for old and young, hearing and Deaf alike!

Swimming

- *Swimming* is an iconic sign using both hands.

- With both hands make the motion as though you were swimming in water.

- Repeat the motion several times.

Breathe

- *Breathe* uses both hands.

- Spread both hands apart and place them on your chest.

- Move the hands away from and back to your chest several times.

- The sign mimics the motion of a chest breathing up and down.

ZOOM

Swimming is a sport that more and more adults are choosing in their quest to be fit for life. Why? Well, first swimming is safe. For bodies that are prone to joint pain, swimming provides a cushioned form of exercise, giving almost a feeling of weightlessness. Second, swimming uses your whole body. Unlike other exercises that tend to develop specific muscle groups, swimming incorporates your whole body and increases your aerobic capacity. When you swim you burn calories at a rate of three calories a mile per pound of body weight. The water environment keeps your body from overheating and provides a very pleasant exercise environment. Swimming can also be an individual sport in which competition is about you and improving your time, your endurance, and your stroke.

Swimming has great psychological benefits as well. It helps develop a good mental attitude and increases self-esteem. Swimming as regular exercise helps increase energy levels and reduces stress. Swimming can also be very therapeutic and relaxing.

Hands

- *Hands* uses both hands.

- Both hands will form the number *5* position.

- Alternately move one hand in front of the other.

Glide

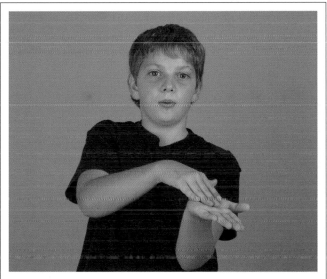

- *Glide* uses both hands.

- The stationary hand will be face up in a number *5* position.

- Using the dominant hand, slowly stroke the stationary hand.

- Begin the stroking motion at the top of the hand toward the fingertips and slowly stroke the hand moving towards the wrist.

BASKETBALL SIGNS

International Deaflympics encourage deaf athletes to soar

In 1924 the International Committee of Sports for the Deaf held the first Deaflympics in Paris. Winter sports were added in 1949 and are sanctioned by the International Olympic Committee. Recognizing that deaf athletes have different communication needs and differentiated social and peer interaction, the committee sought to establish games that would celebrate exceptional deaf athletes in an environment that celebrates their diversity. Deaflympic games differ from

any other IOC-sanctioned games because they cannot use starter guns or whistles. Unlike Olympians, Deaflympians can't just walk up to another athlete and start a conversation or have instant communication. For these reasons, the Deaflympics serve as a place for these exceptional athletes to connect with other athletes. As more and more deaf children are taught in mainstream schools, the games also give deaf students a place to meet and connect with other Deaf. The

Basketball

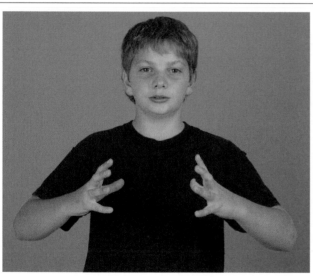

- *Basketball* uses both hands.

- Both palms will be gripping or holding an imaginary ball.

- Alternately move each hand slightly back and forth as though you were feeling the ball.

Move

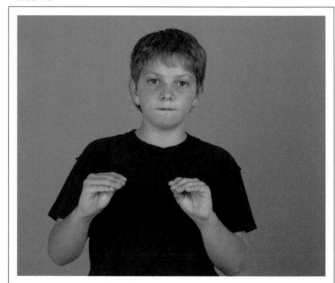

- *Move* uses both hands.

- Begin with both hands closed. The fingertips will touch the thumb, resembling a flat letter *o*.

- Move both hands simultaneously either to the right or to the left in an arc like motion.

- The sign represents the action of something moving.

games are run by deaf people for the deaf athletes.

Today ninety-six national deaf federations are members of the International Committee of Sports for the Deaf. More than three thousand athletes from more than seventy countries participate in the games. The Deaflympics encourage sport opportunities for the Deaf across the globe.

Summer games include athletics, badminton, basketball, beach volleyball, bowling, cycling, karate, judo, shooting, swimming, table tennis, water polo, and wrestling. Winter games include Alpine and cross-country skiing, curling, ice hockey, and snowboarding. The Deaflympics have been held every four years since inception with only one pause during World War II. The twenty-first Summer Deaflympics will be in held in Taipei, Taiwan, in 2009. High Tatras, Slovakia, will host the seventeenth Winter Deaflympics in February 2011. Athens, Greece, will host the twenty-second Summer Deaflympics in 2013.

Here you will learn four important basketball signs: *basketball, move, feet* and *shoot*.

Feet

- *Feet* uses both hands.

- Both hands will be flat and face down.

- One hand will be placed slightly in front of the other.

- Simultaneously and slightly move both hands up and back down to original position, as though the hands or feet were firmly in place.

Shoot

- *Shoot* uses both hands.

- Begin with pretending to hold the ball slightly in front of your face, as though you were about to take a shot.

- Next, move the hands as though you were throwing the ball into the net and taking a shot.

ASKING FOR HELP

In the middle of an emergency, don't be afraid to lend a helping hand

Living in today's society isn't always conducive to helping others. It's understandable. Mounting lawsuits make the most noble of good Samaritans leery of stepping in. Crazy schedules sending people from one place to the next without a moment to spare impede many good intentions. Time, resources, and schedules all affect how willing we are to reach

out when a stranger or even a friend or family member needs help. We shouldn't be so preoccupied with our needs that we forget that helping others is important. So, slow down, remember to be aware of the people around you, and be willing to help.

Conversely, there are times when your help should not

Help

- *Help* is a two-handed sign.

- Form the letter *a* with the dominant hand, thumb facing upward.

- With the other hand, make a flat palm, fingers pressed together. The palm will face upward.

- Place the palm underneath the dominant letter a and move both hands simultaneously upward. The bottom hand is helping the fist move upward.

Emergency

- *Emergency* uses one hand.

- Form the letter *e* with your dominant hand.

- Move the *e* back and forth to the left and right several times.

- Say or mouth *emergency* with a sense of urgency as you sign.

156

be extended. If there is a life-threatening emergency the law requires a certified interpreter. Or, if a deaf person has been arrested, he, too, has the right to a certified interpreter. Although you can help by communicating to emergency personnel that the person is deaf and, with what signs you know, make it clear that you are not qualified to serve as the person's interpreter in these situations.

This chapter will focus on teaching you signs in medical situations that require help. Of course, these are basic signs to help with basic communication and should not substitute for a qualified interpreter. But these signs will help you communicate with the person until an interpreter does arrive. Remember that your body language is going to speak volumes to the deaf person, so try to be calm, to look in control, and to make every effort to communicate whether through signs, gestures, or pen and paper. If you need to ask to call 911, simply sign the numbers *9, 1,* and *1* and make the call sign.

Call

- *Call* can be signed two ways.

- *Call* can be signed by holding an imaginary phone to the side of your head. Extend the pinky and thumb to make it look as though you were talking on a telephone.

- Or, sign *call* by forming a sideways number *1* with the stationary hand.

- Next, form the letter *x* with the dominant hand and run it along the length of the extended finger moving outward.

Ambulance

- *Ambulance* is made using both hands.

- Both hands will be on either side of the shoulders.

- Cup and twist the hands

back and forth, rotating from the wrist.

- The motion symbolizes the flashing and swirling lights on an ambulance.

WHAT'S WRONG?

Be able to effectively determine and communicate the source of the pain

In a medical emergency it is imperative that the caregiver is able to understand what type of pain the patient is feeling. The following signs will help communicate the type of pain the person is experiencing. Again, in an emergency it is imperative that a certified interpreter is present, but interpreters can take minutes to hours to secure. So, it is important to be able to communicate with a deaf person until additional help can arrive.

If you are in an emergency situation, first call 911 and explain that the person who is injured or experiencing pain is deaf and may require an interpreter. Try a couple of signs from earlier chapters that will help you form phrases such as

Pain

- *Pain* uses both hands.

- Form the number *1* with both fingers.

- Begin the motion with both fingers angled toward each other.

- Twist the fingers in alternate directions from the wrist simultaneously.

Hurt

- *Hurt* uses the dominant hand only.

- Form the letter *a* with the thumb pressed against the side of a closed fist.

- Place the *a* on the bottom of the chin.

- Twist the thumb on the chin. Your face should look as if you were hurting.

"Where does it hurt?" by using *where* and *hurt* or *pain*. You can ask the victim to rate the pain on a scale of one to ten. Or have him show you where the pain is. Be aware of potential warning signs such as difficulty in breathing, shortness of breath, fainting, weakness, confusion, change in mental awareness, bleeding that won't stop, or severe vomiting. Be prepared for emergencies by learning CPR and procedures to alleviate choking. Visit your local American Red Cross or American Heart Association to attend classes.

These classes will also teach the basics of first aid so you can stop bleeding and minimize pain until emergency help arrives. If you are untrained in CPR or other medical procedures, don't attempt them. Call 911 first. If a person has been involved in a serious car accident or has fallen and struck his head, it is important not to move the person at all unless the person is in imminent danger. The first few minutes after an injury or crisis are typically the most important, so it's important to be prepared for an emergency.

Bleeding

- *Bleeding* uses both hands.

- The stationary hand will form a fist facing your chest.

- Form a loose number *5* with fingers open with the dominant hand. Place the hand just in front of the closed fist.

- Wiggle the fingers of the dominant hand and move them in a downward direction. The downward movement of the fingers represents something bleeding.

Bruise

- *Bruise* uses the dominant hand.

- Form the letter *I* with the index and thumb extended. All other fingers will be closed.

- Place the *I* over the area that is bruised. For example, as illustrated above, if the bruise is on the upper arm, place the *I* over the upper arm.

- Your face should look as if you were in pain.

GIVING DIRECTIONS
Effective directions and understanding result in a better outcome

Staying calm is one of the most important things a person can do in an emergency. Not panicking, thinking, and acting appropriately make the difference between catastrophe and a medical emergency success story. The following signs will help convey to the victim a sense of well-being and direct him to stay calm.

In the midst of an emergency it is not uncommon to suddenly forget the signs you have seared in your memory. In those cases it is always wise to have a pen and paper handy. If you can't speak the signs with your hands, then write the directions with your pen. If the person is physically able to respond, have her describe in detail what has happened and what she is feeling. To stay calm, she will need to know exactly what is going on. If she sees people talking around her nervously and doesn't know what is being said, her anxiety level will rise. It is important that even the smallest details are conveyed to the

Don't Move

- *Don't move* is a compound sign using both the sign *no* and the sign *move*.

- Shake your head with the *no* back and forth. Say or mouth the word *no* as you sign.

- Close both hands. The fingertips will touch the thumb, resembling a flat letter *o*.

- Move both hands simultaneously either to the right or to the left in an arc like motion.

Stay

- *Stay* uses both hands.

- Form the letter *y* with both hands. The pinky finger and thumb will be extended with the middle three fingers closed.

- Move the hands slightly up and down several times.

- Say or mouth the word *stay* as you sign.

person so that she feels included and is not wondering what is going on around her. The best way for the person to stay calm is to see that you are calm yourself. If possible, distract the person with other conversation until help arrives.

Calm

- *Calm* uses both hands.

- Begin with both palms flat and crossed, forming an x shape.

- The palms will be crossed just in front of your mouth.

- Draw the two palms away from one another until the palms are facing downward.

Okay

- *Okay* uses the dominant hand.

- You will use the abbreviation *o* and *k* for the word.

- Begin with first forming the letter *o* and then the letter *k*.

- Say *o* and *k* as you sign the letters. If you are asking if the person is okay, your face should reflect concern.

AT THE HOSPITAL

Help reduce hospital anxiety with proper preparation, comfort, and care

Waiting in an emergency room is never fun. The smell of a hospital alone is unnerving, but combined with the strange sights and the hard seats, the seemingly endless wait exacerbates the emergency you are in. The hospital, although it may not seem like it at the time, is doing its best to see and treat you or your loved one. If you are helping a deaf friend or loved one at the hospital, spend that time taking care of business. Obtain all of the forms needed and begin to help that person fill them out. See if you can provide comfort or relief through food, coffee, or water. If the television is not showing captions, ask the hospital to turn on the captions. When it is time for your loved one to be seen, be sure that the hospital

The ADA and Communication

- The Americans with Disabilities Act requires that effective communication be provided for families and patients who are deaf.

- If the situation warrants an interpreter, he or she must be a qualified and certified interpreter to ensure that the signing is accurate, complete, and without bias.

- Hospitals may not charge the patient or the family for the interpreter services.

Doctor

- *Doctor* uses both hands.

- Turn the stationary hand upward and hold it still in a flat position.

- Form a broken palm with the dominant hand.

- Strike the fingertips several times against the base of the stationary palm.

staff is aware the person is deaf so that effective communication can be provided.

Effective communication will look different for each person, depending on how much hearing the person has, his ability to speech read, and his comfort with written communication. Effective communication may require the use of an interpreter, which is at the sole discretion of the deaf person. The patient could be the child of deaf parents, and effective communication for the deaf parents will still be required so that they are able to make informed decisions. As your friend's advocate, ensure that his concerns and requests are being heard.

Here you will learn three hospital basics: *doctor, nurse,* and *insurance.*

Nurse

- *Nurse* uses both hands. The sign is very similar to the sign for *doctor.*

- Turn the stationary hand upward and hold it still in a flat position.

- Instead of using a broken palm, you will use an upside-down *u* shape with the dominant hand.

- Strike the tips of the fingers against the base of the stationary palm several times.

Insurance

- *Insurance* uses the dominant hand only.

- Form the letter *i* with the pinky finger extended. All other fingers will remain closed.

- Move the *i* side to side from the wrist several times.

THE WAITING ROOM

Before even leaving to see the doctor, help your loved one prepare

Seeing the doctor can be stressful. Being concerned about a specific ailment or pain, coupled with the wait time and the concern that perhaps what the patient is feeling won't be communicated effectively, can make any patient nervous. For the Deaf, communicating exactly what is wrong can be especially difficult. If you are taking your deaf family member or friend to the doctor, consider suggesting that your loved one do the following to ensure the best doctor visit possible:

Before the appointment, make some lists. On one list include any medications currently being taken and why, including vitamins. Then make a list of symptoms, how long the symptoms have existed, what the discomfort level of those symptoms is on a scale from one to ten, and the treatments tried. Last, bring a list of questions you want to ask the doctor.

If your loved one already has all of this information written or printed out ahead of time, it will make communication

Waiting

- *Waiting* uses both hands.

- Face both palms, fingers apart toward your body.

- Wiggle your fingers back and forth.

- If you are using waiting in the context of having to wait a long time, your face will look tired or irritated.

Room

- *Room* uses both hands. You will make two distinct motions in this sign.

- Both hands will remain in the same shape throughout the sign. Form the number *5* and turn the hands sideways.

- The first part of the sign is both hands placed one in front of each other horizontally.

- Next, move the hands so that they are side by side vertically. This forms the shape of a square or room.

that much easier for both the patient and the doctor.

Next, make sure the patient arrives slightly early or on time for the doctor visit. Arriving on time helps the doctor stay on schedule throughout the day.

If you are accompanying a deaf friend or loved one to the appointment, be sure to ask if he understands what is being said. If not, have a pen and paper handy for questions and explanations. When speaking to the doctor, be concise with the details. Don't waste time on information that isn't relevant to why you are at the appointment. If the deaf person has concerns about

communication ahead of time, request that an interpreter be present before the appointment. It is always a good idea to have an additional set of ears to hear, ask questions, and understand what the doctor is communicating. If you can't be there for your friend, encourage him or her to bring someone along to ensure important information is understood.

Fill Out

- *Fill out* uses both hands.

- The stationary hand will act as the tablet or form that you are filling out. Keep it flat and still.

- The dominant hand represents the information or words that will go on the form.

- Move the dominant hand from the top of the hand to the bottom as though you were filling out information line by line.

Form

- *Form* uses both hands.

- Form the letter *f* with both hands. The thumb and index fingers will touch, with all other fingers open and extended.

- Begin with the hands about shoulder level.

- Move the hands downward to indicate the length of a form. Say or mouth the word *form* as you sign the word.

UNDERSTANDING THE TREATMENT

Being an informed patient helps both patient and doctor

As a patient, you know your body better than anyone else. Although you may be seeing a specialist or medical practitioner who excels in her field, you are still the best expert on your body. So, it is always a good idea to self-inform as much as possible. If you are the loved one of a deaf person, encourage the deaf person to make himself as informed as possible. It's scary to get informed. Doing a search on the Internet about any symptom is enough to induce a panic attack. Yet, mud-

dling through the information can help you learn more about possible causes and treatments. The time you take to inform yourself is worth the investment. Remember that you and your doctor want the same outcome—a healthier patient!

As a patient or loved one of a patient, recognize that a doctor will not always be the right fit for what you are going through at the time. For example, surgery is going to be the likely suggested treatment if a surgeon is the only doctor

Hospital

- *Hospital* uses the dominant hand.

- Form the letter *u* using the index and middle finger extended. All other fingers will be closed.

- Just below the shoulder of the passive arm, stroke the *u* downward in a straight line on the arm.

- Next, stroke the *u* across the arm to form a cross or a letter t on the arm.

Operation

- *Operation* uses both hands.

- The passive hand will be flat and perpendicular to your body.

- Form the letter *a* with the dominant hand extending the thumb beside the closed fingers.

- Glide the thumb of the *a* down the palm of the hand, much like an incision that is made during surgery.

consulted. Alternative therapies or treatments may not even be considered because they affect his income stream or may involve treatments he is uneducated about. Or your doctor may not know what specifically the best fit is for you and your preferences. At the same time don't let your emotion or uncertainty keep you from asking questions and exploring the best care for you.

Helping your deaf friend or loved one research, ask questions, and be informed will make the doctor-patient relationship more beneficial to both. The more information one has and the more in control of one's health one feels, the less anxiety and stress one is going to have in the doctor's office. It pays to be informed! Here, you'll learn the signs for *hospital, operation, draw blood,* and *shot.*

Draw Blood

- *Draw blood* uses both hands.

- Place your passive arm in a position as though someone were about to take blood from your arm.

- Next, place the dominant hand close to the bend of the elbow. Begin with the hand slightly open and apart.

- Pull the dominant hand away from the arm, closing the hand. This is representative of a needle taking blood.

Shot

- *Shot* uses the dominant hand.

- Form the letter *l* with the thumb and index finger extended. All other fingers are closed.

- Place the fingertip of the index finger on the arm, representing the needle of a syringe.

- Press down the thumb, representing the injection of the shot.

DIAGNOSIS & EXPLANATIONS

Take the time and effort to ensure your deaf patient understands

Doctor, do you have deaf patients? If so, you've already discovered that they are like every other patient you have: nervous, full of questions and concerns, and perhaps anxious about understanding. Helping your patient to understand everything from blood pressure to diagnosis and treatment is essential. The ADA requires that your office or hospital provide effective communication to this individual. If this requires the use of an interpreter, be sure to arrange one ahead

of time. Failing to secure proper communication methods can be a liability to your office and a potential lawsuit. Avoid this liability by ensuring that your office provides effective communication.

Before your patient returns, ask that the patient bring with him written questions he has. When communicating the answer, be as thorough as possible, describing as much detail and information as you can. Ask repeatedly if the patient un-

Take

- *Take* uses the dominant hand.

- Reach the hand out toward an imaginary object that you would like to take.

- Pull the hand back, closing the hand into a fist. The hand is closed as though you had just taken an item and were now holding it in your fist.

Blood Pressure

- *Blood pressure* uses the passive arm and the dominant hand.

- Cup the dominant hand around the upper passive arm.

- This iconic sign represents the cuff of a blood pressure monitor on the arm.

derstands. If specific directions were issued, have the patient repeat the directions to be sure that nothing was lost in translation. Do not sugarcoat or minimize the information. Before the patient leaves, write down or print out the key points of what was discussed, leaving no room for misunderstanding.

If you use an interpreter, be sure your conversation is pointed not at the interpreter but directly at the patient. Speak to the patient clearly so that if possible the patient will be able to speech read as you speak. If possible, sit down with your patient, making her feel as though you aren't rushed and that her concerns are important to you. Last, have a follow-up plan for deaf patients. Give them written instructions of what to do should a problem arise after hours, how to contact the office, and what the plan is until the next appointment. Use relay services, e-mail, and text messaging to remind the patient of the next appointment.

Temperature

- *Temperature* uses both hands.

- Form the number *1* with both hands. The index finger will be the only extended finger.

- The passive hand will have a straight-up-and-down *1*.

- Turn the dominant finger horizontally and place the finger on top of the passive finger. Slide the finger up and down much like a reading on a thermometer.

Test

- *Test* uses both hands.

- Form the letter *x* with each hand. Place the hands about shoulder level.

- This symmetrical sign will simultaneously move the hands downward.

- As you move the *x* downward, wiggle the *x* back and forth.

DESCRIBING PAIN
Understand Deaf rights under the Americans with Disabilities Act

The Americans with Disabilities Act was enacted by Congress in 1990. This legislation was designed to prohibit discrimination in the workplace, public accommodations, medical facilities, transportation, and telecommunication. By definition under the ADA, the disabled are those persons who have a physical or mental disability that limits one or more major life activities. This legislation has had a profound impact on the life of the disabled. For Deaf Americans, the

legislation has most affected two areas: workplace discrimination and accommodation and guarantee of effective medical communication.

The guarantee of effective medical communication has been important. No longer are the Deaf reliant on family members or friends to interpret or to guess what the medical provider was communicating. This is important because not all family members or friends are qualified to interpret. Imagine a

Medical Rights for the Deaf

• The Americans with Disabilities Act is a federal civil rights law protecting the rights of disabled Americans.

• The ADA requires effective communication for the Deaf in all medical situations.

• The Deaf cannot be charged a fee by the hospital or medical provider for effective communication services, including the services of an interpreter.

Show

• *Show* uses both hands.

• The stationary palm will be flat, straight, and facing outward.

• The dominant hand will form the number *1*, with all fingers but the index finger closed.

• Place the finger on the bottom of the palm.

• Together, move both the finger and the palm outward.

young child trying to translate medical words and phrases that the child doesn't understand. Or unqualified siblings or children may leave out information they deem unimportant or answer questions without first interpreting the question or incorrectly sign the conversation. Or, in emotionally charged medical situations, information may not be properly communicated or may be omitted while the family member is trying to absorb what has just occurred. These miscommunications can be dangerous or lead to a misdiagnosis. In addition to the danger of miscommunication, they force the family member or child to function as the interpreter instead of providing emotional support and comfort.

It is essential that in warranted situations qualified interpreters are present to ensure that proper diagnosis, treatment, and follow-up are provided. By law, medical personnel must provide effective communication. Effective communication will look different, depending on the severity of the hearing loss, the ability to speech read, the ability to communicate via paper and pen, and the severity of the medical issue.

What Is?

- *What is?* is made using both hands.

- Form each hand in the letter *g* position, palm facing upward.

- Place each hand about waist level, about shoulder width apart.

- Move the index finger back and forth over the thumb several times. Make sure your facial expression looks as though you are asking the question.

Wrong

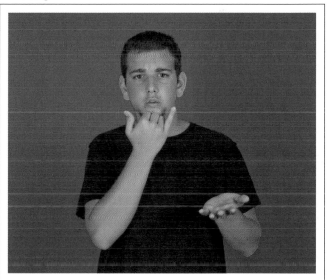

- *Wrong* uses both hands.

- The passive palm will be flat, palm facing upward.

- The dominant hand will form the letter *y* with the pinky and thumb extended.

- All other fingers will be closed.

- Place the *y* on the bottom of your chin, fingers facing your body. Move the *y* on and off the bottom of your chin several times.

171

SIGNS & SYMPTOMS

Signs for common sicknesses help you understand what is wrong

Sore throat, diarrhea, nausea, throwing up— yikes, those all sound like symptoms of the flu or a bad virus. If you work in a doctor's office you are likely to be surrounded by these symptoms daily. Understanding what the patient is describing to you will help you diagnose and treat the patient sooner.

According to www.flufacts.com, about 25 to 50 million Americans report contracting the flu every year. Of those, 30,000 to 40,000 die every year from flu or complications

from the flu. Preventing the flu is obviously the primary goal. How can you help your patients avoid this nasty sickness?

Getting the flu shot is the first line of defense. In the autumn, the flu vaccine becomes available and should be administered as soon as possible. The vaccine can be administered by an injection or nasally. The flu vaccine protects against the three main flu strains that are at most risk of causing infection. People who are at high risk for serious flu complica-

Sore Throat

- *Sore throat* uses the dominant hand.

- Form the letter *g* with the index and thumb extended. All other fingers are closed.

- Beginning at the top of your throat, just under-neath your chin, place the tips of the *g*.

- Next, move the fingers in a downward motion the length of your neck. Your face should look as though you don't feel well.

Diarrhea

- *Diarrhea* uses both hands.

- Although it isn't pleasant, it is a symptom the doctor should be aware of. The passive hand will be an open palm, pinky toward the ground.

- Form an open number *5* with all fingers slightly apart. Begin with touching the bottom of the palm.

- Move the hand downward and wiggle the hand back and forth slightly.

tions, such as the elderly, young children, pregnant women, or those with chronic health conditions, should always get the flu shot.

The signs shown below will help you as you communicate with a sick patient, or if you yourself are the patient and need to communicate with the doctor or nurse.

Nausea

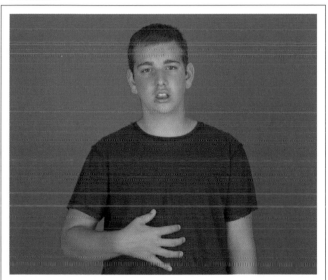

- *Nausea* can be made with one or two hands.

- Place the hand or hands on the stomach.

- Move the hand in a circular motion.

- Your facial expression should look like you feel very sick.

Throw Up

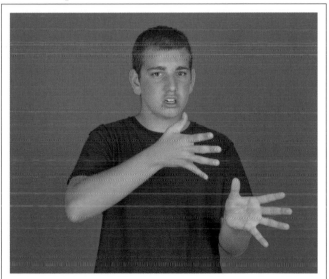

- *Throw up* uses both hands.

- Both hands will be in open number *5* positions with the fingers slightly apart.

- Stagger one hand slightly higher than the other.

- Move the hands outward, imitating the motion of throwing up.

SERIOUS MEDICAL CONDITIONS

Learn to communicate with loved ones who may be seriously incapacitated

A loved one's final days can be especially frustrating for both the Deaf and their family members. Many times the care of the patient encumbers the use of her hands and voice. Without the ability to hear, the patient is not able to communicate or know what is being said. Such patients are especially at risk of feeling isolated and of not being able to communicate what they need

in the final days. Effective communication between doctor, patient, and family members is essential in the final days of care. For this reason, Deaf hospice services exist across the country to give the Deaf the best care in their final days. These caregivers are trained in ASL and oral methods and have the sensitivity to understand the smallest use of gestures and sign.

Cancer

- *Cancer* uses both hands.

- The stationary hand is flat, palm facing upward.

- The dominant hand forms the letter *c*.

- The motion begins at the base of the wrist and moves forward along the hand. The *c* opens and closes, symbolic of how cancer eats away at the body.

Heart

- *Heart* can be signed two ways.

- As shown, with one hand lightly tap the area over your heart with the dominant middle finger.

- Or, with both hands, draw a heart on the chest. Use the middle fingers of both hands to trace the heart shape beginning at the top of the heart.

When a patient has run out of treatment options, and a cure is no longer possible, many families turn to a hospice for care of their loved one. Hospice care is performed under the care of the patient's doctor and in home, where the patient is more comfortable and surrounded by the ones he loves. It is usually considered time for hospice when the treatment for the patient is no longer working or there are no longer treatment options.

When treatment will only postpone the end and not enhance the quality of life in those last days and when the patient is having difficulty eating or breathing, is in considerable pain, and is sleeping for a large part of the day, it may be time for hospice.

Disease

- *Disease* uses both hands.

- With the middle finger of each hand extended, place the tip on the middle of the chest.

- Move each hand simultaneously in alternate directions back and forth.

- Your facial expression should look very ill.

Stroke

- *Stroke* uses the dominant hand only.

- Begin by forming the number *1* and pointing it toward the head.

- Next, change the hand to a flat, slightly curved palm and touch it to the head.

STAYING HEALTHY

DISABILITIES
Being deaf with compound disabilities can make life more challenging

Being deaf in a hearing world is not always easy. Yet, for many Deaf, not hearing is only the beginning of what they must battle every day. Many Deaf must overcome other disabilities, such as blindness, cerebral palsy, mental retardation, autism, and learning disabilities. Many wonder how people can overcome such challenges. Yet, every day these courageous individuals show how able they are.

Although autistic children who are also deaf are not common, they do exist. Because many children who are autistic do not respond to voices, sometimes deafness is not initially recognized. With early detection, children who have been diagnosed with autism and who are deaf have the potential to do very well.

Blind

- *Blind* is made using the dominant hand.

- Form the letter *v* with the index and middle fingers extended and spread apart. No other fingers should be extended.

- Place the tips of the *v* inches away from your eyes. Straddle the *v* so that one finger is on either side of the nose.

- Move the *v* slightly in and out to say blind.

Deaf

- *Deaf* is made with the dominant hand.

- Form the letter *d* with the middle finger touching the thumb and index finger extended. The ring and pinky fingers are closed.

- Begin with the *d* on the side of your chin.

- Move the *d* backward in an arc motion to rest just below the ear.

Cerebral palsy (CP) is a condition in which damage has occurred to the brain during development in pregnancy, during the birthing process, or during infancy. The damage affects muscle coordination and body movements. CP is not a disease and cannot be cured, but with therapy, muscle function and coordination can be improved.

A person who is deaf and blind probably has some hearing or some vision or some of both. About half of those who are deaf and blind are so because of the genetic condition known as "Usher syndrome." Others may be deaf and blind because of glaucoma, macular degeneration, birth trauma, accidents, illnesses, or other causes. Deaf and blind people can still speak and read through ASL within their range of sight, tactile sign language, finger spelling, Braille, and print on palm or other methods, depending on the amount and severity of the sight and hearing loss. Despite the obstacles facing the deaf-blind, many have very active and productive lives and careers. These individuals are teachers, counselors, business owners, students, and more. Those who are multiply disabled face greater challenges but are not without support or hope.

Glasses

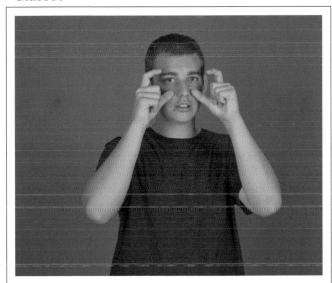

- *Glasses* uses both hands.

- Form a *c* shape with both hands, except fold the middle, fourth, and pinky fingers closed.

- Bring the hands to the outside of either eye, symbolizing glasses.

Wheelchair

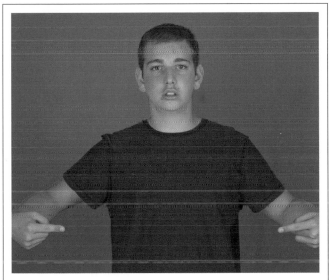

- *Wheelchair* is a symmetrical sign using both hands.

- Form the number *1* with both hands.

- At about chest level, move the fingers in a circular motion.

- Make several circles, symbolic of the wheels on a wheelchair.

DOCTOR'S ORDERS

Proper communication and follow through help the patient better follow the doctor's instructions

Now that the appointment is over, how can you ensure that the patient understands and can reach the doctor's office in case of question?

Before the patient leaves the office, make sure he has complete understanding of what has just occurred. You may decide to recap the visit by following up with a written or printed synopsis of the doctor's visit. Include any instructions that were given verbally and make sure the patient reads the sheet and understands everything. If a patient needs to make follow-up visits, lab appointments, or appointments with a specialist, detail exactly what the patient must accomplish and what the office will take care of, eliminating any confu-

Patient Communication Basics

• How will the patient be able to reach you in an emergency? Is your office prepared to accept relay calls? Can the patient e-mail questions? Have an effective communication method in place before an emergency occurs.

• How will you communicate test results? If possible, find a way to speak directly to the patient, not the patient's child, sibling, or parent. Use a relay service or e-mail the patient for one-to-one communication.

Understand

• *Understand* uses the dominant hand only.

• Begin with the index finger and thumb forming an *o* shape. All other fingers will be closed.

• Place your hand near the temple on the same side as the arm you are using to sign with.

• With the fingers facing the temple, flick the fingers apart.

sion. Finally, if the patient has had tests performed, specifically inform the patient of when results can be expected.

Provide an e-mail address for the patient to communicate concerns or encourage the patient to call the office using relay services. It is not uncommon for patients to leave an office forgetting to ask a key question. For the Deaf, it is especially difficult to make that quick call and have the nurse return the call. So having e-mail communication available helps ease the communication barrier between patient and doctor. If the patient does not agree with the suggested treatment, then give him options and encourage him to seek a second opinion.

Before the patient returns for the next visit, encourage him to do his homework ahead of time and be prepared for the visit. Ensure that the doctor's office has done its homework, too, by allowing ample time for the visit and setting up any interpreter services that may be needed.

Here you will learn three signs to help your office visit go more smoothly: *understand, rest* and *prescription/medicine*.

Rest

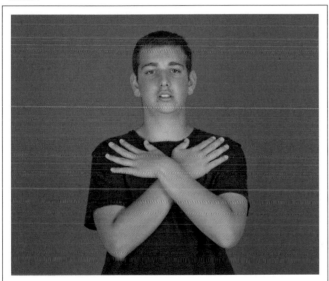

- *Rest* uses both hands.

- Cross both arms across the chest forming a large *x* shape.

- The hands will be open palmed with fingers slightly apart.

- Be careful not to form closed fists with your hands, or else you'll be saying *love* instead of *rest*.

Prescription or Medicine

- You will use both hands to form this sign.

- The passive hand will represent the tablet the doctor would write the prescription on. The hand is still, and the palm is facing upward.

- Place the middle finger of the dominant hand on the center of the open passive palm.

- Move the middle finger slightly back and forth without moving it from the center of the palm.

179

OFFICE ESSENTIALS
Arrange a user-friendly working environment for your deaf employees

How is the office arranged? This may seem like a silly question to most people. What difference does it make where the desk or computer is situated? Having a Deaf user-friendly office usually involves only rearranging some office essentials. For example, consider where a desk is placed for the deaf employee. The desk should be faced so that the front of the per-

son is facing the door, cubicle opening, or co-workers who may enter the room. By being able to see who enters his area, the deaf worker is able to be responsive and not be startled by someone sneaking up behind him. Is there a light switch or a lamp or other light that can be flickered on and off to grab his attention? If not, place a lamp in the office or place

Computer

- *Computer* uses both the passive arm and the dominant hand.

- Hold the passive arm in front of you with the palm facing downward.

- Form the letter *c* with the dominant hand.

- Brush the *c* against the forearm several times.

E-mail

- *E-mail* uses both hands.

- The passive hand forms the letter *c*.

- Form the letter *e* with the dominant hand.

- Move the *e* through the *c* while twisting the wrist.

his work area near a light switch. These easy gestures can immediately grab a deaf person's attention. Similarly, place key office equipment such as the fax machine, the copier, and the printer in such a way that when a person is using it her back is not facing the door or entry. In the hearing world, we take for granted the little noises that alert us to others in the room—footsteps, hallway chatter, even a cough. Without these hearing cues, a deaf person relies on his eyes to hear for him. Make the job easier by carefully considering how these office essentials are arranged.

YELLOW LIGHT

No surprises! When you walk into a deaf person's office, make sure he knows you are there. Don't stand around waiting to be noticed. Instead, either flick the light switch on and off, or, if no light exists, walk over to the person and lightly tap him on the arm. Avoid big movements or a hearty pounding on the back. You don't want to scare the person; you just want to let him know you have something to say.

Fax

- *Fax* uses both hands.

- The stationary hand will be a slightly curved palm. This hand will not move.

- Move the dominant palm underneath the stationary palm.

- The motion represents a piece of paper being sent through a fax machine.

Copy

- *Copy* is made using both hands.

- The passive hand will be a flat palm, facing downward.

- The dominant hand will begin by having all fingers touch the bottom of the palm.

- Draw the fingers away from the hand and close the fingers together.

181

PLACES & SPACES
Understand how the ADA impacts your working environment

It is always smart for an employer to have open discussions with a disabled employee to see how to best accommodate that person. When an employee feels that the workplace is not providing "reasonable accommodations," he may file a complaint with the Equal Employment Opportunity Commission. If a company fails to comply with Title I regulations, it is creating a potentially liable environment and may be at risk for legal action. As an employer, being proactive and creating

an environment that seeks to make accommodation a priority will not only help your employee but also will deliver the message that you care not just about the work but also the employee. An employee who feels valued and appreciated will be a more efficient and productive employee.

In this section you will learn four signs that are integral to any business setting: *office, human resources, elevator* and *mail.*

Office

- *Office* uses both hands.

- Form the letter *o* with both hands. All fingers will be touching the thumb.

- Cross the wrists so they form an x shape as shown above. The inside of your

wrists will be facing your body.

- Next, rotate your wrists and arms while uncrossing your arms. The sign ends with each *o* apart and facing downward.

H.R. or Human Resources

- *H.R.* uses the dominant hand.

- First, form the letter *h* with the index and middle fingers extended. All other fingers are closed.

- Next, form the letter *r* with the middle finger crossed over the index finger.

- The letters *h* and *r* form *H.R.* or *human resources.*

ZOOM

Title I of the Americans with Disabilities Act gives specific protection to the disabled. It requires that employers with fifteen or more employees make "reasonable accommodations" in the workplace for the limitations of the disabled employee. What does that mean for a deaf person? It means that the work environment needs to be adapted so that the deaf employee is at the same advantage as hearing employees.

For the deaf, communication is the greatest barrier at work, so reasonable accommodations would include having TTYs or TDDs (the equipment for the deaf to talk over the telephone) or telephones with volume loud enough for a hard-of-hearing person to hear. There should also be ways of alerting the deaf person of fire or other emergency through flashing lights. Additionally, when the situation merits an interpreter—for example, reviews, computer or software training, or explanation of change in benefits—one should be provided. The amount of help or accommodation necessary will depend on the individual.

Elevator

- *Elevator* uses both hands.

- The passive hand is a flat, vertical palm and does not move.

- The dominant hand forms the letter *e* with all four fingers resting on the thumb.

- Slide the *e* up and down the length of the open palm, indicating an elevator moving up and down.

Mail

- *Mail* uses both hands.

- The stationary hand will be palm up, flat, and not moving.

- The dominant hand will be in the letter *a* position.

- Begin the sign with the *a* brushing your lips, almost as if you had just licked a stamp.

- Next, firmly place the thumb on the open palm as though you were affixing a stamp to an envelope.

A DAY OFF
Take advantage of holidays or vacations to start a great conversation

Although not everyone may know ASL or have been around the Deaf before, having a deaf co-worker is a great reason to learn. Employers and managers are the example to which other employees look. Set a good example by actively reaching out and learning how to communicate with the Deaf.

There are great ways to be living examples. First, have several ASL dictionaries handy where the staff can easily access them, perhaps in the break room or cafeteria, in the lobby, or in areas such as the copy center where other resources are stored. Having easy access to the dictionary will help people quickly and easily look up a sign to communicate. Second, set the example of how to talk to the deaf person by looking at him, using gestures and sign, and making an effort. Don't allow several simultaneous conversations to occur. Instead make it a point to guide employees to make sure they are including the deaf person in the conversation. Don't carry

Vacation

- *Vacation* uses both hands.

- Form an open number *5* with both hands. Fingers will be slightly spread apart.

- Place the thumbs below your shoulders.

- Simultaneously move the hands away from and to the body again slightly. This is not a big movement. The thumb will just come off the body before touching it again. Repeat this motion several times.

Holiday

- *Holiday* uses both hands.

- Form an open number *5* with both hands. Fingers will be slightly spread apart.

- Place the thumbs of the open number *5* at the armpits.

- Wiggle the extended fingers around.

on conversations in the break room, hallway, or other places in front of the deaf person without including him. Do team-building activities that encourage other methods of communication besides hearing. Use e-mail for communication as much as possible. Setting a good example will encourage everyone to be better communicators.

When someone has been away from the office it is normal to ask how he has been. Be able to talk about vacation, holidays, breaks, and being sick with these four signs.

Break

- *Break* uses both hands.

- Slide the flat palm of the dominant hand in between the fingers of the passive hand.

- *Break* also can be signed by holding an invisible stick with both hands.

- Next, pretend to break the stick in half. This version of *break* would be indicative of something that is broken.

Sick

- *Sick* is made using both hands.

- The dominant hand will be on the forehead, and the other hand will be on the chest.

- Each hand will be making the same motion. The middle fingers will be extended, touching either the head or chest, with the other fingers spread apart.

- As you touch your forehead or chest, slightly collapse your chest as though you felt terrible.

BENEFITS
What to expect as an employer when using an interpreter

Most of the time an interpreter will not be needed to communicate with your deaf co-worker or employee. However, there are times when an interpreter should be present. Family members of the deaf employee should not be considered as interpreters. First, they would be providing your company a service without compensation. Second, family members may not be qualified to interpret. They might not translate everything that was spoken, might make assumptions for the deaf person, or might answer questions that they have not been authorized to answer. Last, asking the deaf person to provide his own translator is not complying with providing reasonable accommodation for the deaf worker as required by Title I of the ADA. When discussing important events such as reviews, changes in benefit programs, or introduction of benefit programs, retirement, and layoffs, accurate communication of information is imperative.

Retire

- *Retire* uses both hands.

- Form the letter *I* with both hands.

- Place the thumb in the armpit, much like the sign for holiday.

- Move the thumb on and off the body several times. The motion is not large, and the thumb should just barely come off the body before being placed back on.

Insurance

- *Insurance* uses the dominant hand only.

- Form the letter *i* with the pinky finger extended. All other fingers will remain closed.

- Move the *i* side to side from the wrist several times.

The qualified interpreter will provide a great service to both the company and the employee. As an employer you should expect the interpreter to be on time and to be professional. The interpreter should be made aware ahead of time of any company policies or procedures such as a dress code or other issues that may affect her role. She keeps your discussions confidential. The interpreter will do her job to interpret and only interpret. The interpreter will not answer for or make assumptions for the employee, or arbitrarily decide what information should and should not be communicated.

Profit

- *Profit* uses the dominant hand only.

- Form the letter *f*.

- Act as though the *f* were money, or profit, that you are putting into your pocket.

- Move the *f* slightly up and down, touching your waist or imaginary pocket.

Sharing

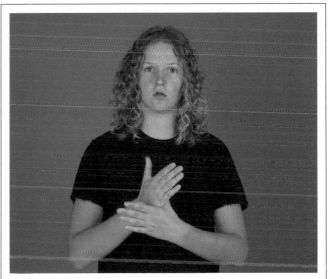

- *Sharing* uses both hands.

- The passive hand will be horizontal palm facing upward. This hand will not move.

- The dominant hand is in a closed number *5* position. The fingers are close together, with only the thumb extended.

- Place the dominant hand on its side on top of the passive hand. Move the hand back and forth. The motion represents splitting something in half or down the middle.

REVIEWS & EVALUATIONS

A review helps both employee and employer chart a future path

Evaluation time is important for both the employer and the employee. It gives both parties a time to reflect on the past year, the goals, and how well the goals were reached. It is a time to celebrate the successes of great performances and to discuss what could have been done better. Looking forward, evaluation time allows the employer and the employee to get on the same page and set goals to work toward. Many companies require employees to get involved actively in the review process by giving a review to themselves and/or others in their group. Involving the employee allows the employer to see areas that the employee feels successful in that might not have been otherwise recognized. It also gives an opportunity for frustrations to be discussed.

When evaluating a deaf employee, be sure to give notice of what is going to happen before the evaluation. If there are reports to be read, furnish the reports ahead of time so

Review

- *Review* uses both hands.

- The passive hand will be in a vertical number *5* position. The thumb will face your body.

- The dominant hand forms the letter *r* with the thumb extended as well. The fourth and fifth fingers are closed.

- Place the thumb on the center of the passive palm. Begin with the *r* straight up and down. From the wrist, rotate the *r* downward away from your body.

Raise

- *Raise* uses both hands.

- Form the letter *h* with both hands. The index and middle fingers will be the only fingers extended. All other fingers will be closed.

- The passive *h* is horizontal, and the palm will face down.

- The dominant *h* begins face up, at the same level and close by the passive *h*.

- Rotate the *h* to sit on top of the passive *h*. Both hands will now be palm down.

188

that the employee can prepare and ask questions. If the employee must do a self-evaluation, review the questions with the employee, being sure the employee has a complete understanding of what is expected from her.

A common complaint from many deaf workers is the inability to advance in their career. Many deaf workers feel like they are "stuck" in positions because of communication barriers. In the review, consider how the employee can continue to advance within the company and offer direct and concrete steps that the employee can take for career advancement.

Be sure to allot enough time for the employee and you to discuss key issues, points, and questions. After a time of reflection and goal setting both you and the employee will feel good about the year to come.

Evaluation

- *Evaluation* uses both hands.

- Form the letter *e* with both hands. The fingers will be bent touching the thumb.

- Begin with one *e* slightly higher than the other.

- Move both hands alternately up and down. When one hand is up, the other will be down. Repeat the motion several times.

Test

- *Test* is made using both hands.

- Form the number *1* with both hands.

- Begin with the hands at about shoulder level.

- Wiggle the extended fingers as both hands move simultaneously downward several inches.

INDUSTRIES

Keep all of your employees in a safe working environment

Workplace safety is a concern for all employees and employers. Having an action plan helps alleviate stress, injury, and loss of life in the event of an emergency. If you have a deaf employee, be sure to review any emergency plans to be sure the deaf worker is included. Consider creating a buddy system for work. Give the deaf worker a partner to be sure that in the event of an emergency these two people are responsible for communicating with one another. Install flashing alarm lights in conjunction with any fire or safety alarm system. For routine communication, use e-mail. Avoid verbally distributing pertinent company business. Use e-mail to ensure that everyone has a written copy of office announcements. Be sure that the closed captioning function of the television is turned on. In the event of a weather or national security emergency, it is imperative that the deaf person be able to read the latest news.

Discrimination in the Workplace

- Does deaf discrimination occur at work? Intentional discrimination is usually rare, but unintentional discrimination does occur:

- A deaf person is given the tasks no one else wants. Many Deaf complain that their work is below their ability, skill, and education level.

- A deaf person is left out of meetings or chatter.

- A hearing person assumes that a deaf person cannot complete a task because of an inability to talk on a telephone.

Law

- *Law* uses both hands.

- The passive hand will be in a vertical number *5* position. The thumb will face your body.

- The dominant hand will form the letter *l* for law.

- Begin with the *l* at the top of the passive hand. Then, in an arc like motion, move the *l* to the bottom of the palm.

Heavy equipment in the workplace should also use established paths of travel. The noise of the forklift will not be enough to alert a deaf person that he may be in the path. Lights and mirrors on the equipment should be utilized to increase awareness of both the driver and passerby. Designating vehicle-only doors for traffic will also reduce risk. If the employee has a service dog, the dog will also help alert the person of potential dangers, sounds, or alarms. In the event of power loss, have flashlights accessible to help the person speech read or sign in the dark.

By using just a little common sense and thinking through safety issues, the workplace can be a safe and injury-free facility for all employees. Don't be afraid to ask the deaf employee for her suggestions to better your work environment.

Here you will learn three signs for three types of industries: *law, business,* and *manufacturing*. Use these signs to describe what you do, what others do or companies your industry may interact with.

Business

- *Business* uses the dominant hand and the passive arm.

- The passive arm will be placed horizontally in front of your body. The hand will be flat, fingers together, palm facing down.

- The dominant hand will form the letter *b* for *business*.

- Sweep the *b* back and forth against the wrist area several times.

Manufacture

- *Manufacture* uses both hands.

- Form the letter *s* with both hands.

- Place the dominant fist on top of the passive fist.

- From the wrist, pull each fist backward away from one another. The dominant fist will still be above passive fist.

191

MAKING SMALL TALK
Reach out and get to know your deaf co-worker

Getting to know a deaf co-worker is a great reason to learn ASL. Learning ASL and having the ability to communicate with this person will remove the awkward moments. Equipped with ASL, no longer will you feel the embarrassment of not knowing what to do, if your gestures make sense, or if the person understands you. Your efforts to try to communicate will also show your deaf co-worker that you are making an effort at being a friend, not just an acquaintance who smiles as

you pass one another. The coffee machine, the copy machine, and the elevator are all great places to try new phrases. Here you will learn the phrase *Did you have a good week?* Practice an answer to this question. It will likely be asked back to you. Go back to earlier chapters and review phrases and questions to ask your co-worker. Practicing these phrases ahead of time and having fluency when you are alone will help you when it is show time. You'll be less likely to suddenly forget the sign

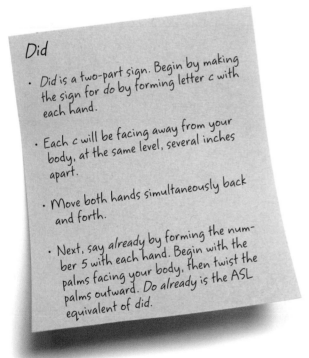

Did

- *Did* is a two-part sign. Begin by making the sign for *do* by forming letter *c* with each hand.

- Each *c* will be facing away from your body, at the same level, several inches apart.

- Move both hands simultaneously back and forth.

- Next, say *already* by forming the number 5 with each hand. Begin with the palms facing your body, then twist the palms outward. *Do already* is the ASL equivalent of *did*.

Have

- *Have* uses both hands.

- Each hand will form a bent palm. Fingers are close together, with the thumb extended.

- Place the tips of each palm on your chest.

and instead will look like a seasoned signer.

If several people begin to join in the conversation, indicate which person said what by pointing to that person. Remind the others to not turn their back toward the deaf person and when asking questions to look at the person and not at you, if you are the one interpreting or attempting to interpret. Be mindful of where you are standing. For example, don't stand and sign where a glare is cast onto your body, making it difficult to see what is being said. Avoid chewing gum or snacking while conversing. The snacking and gum can be too distracting to the person to whom you are signing. Also consider removing sunglasses so the person you are speaking to can see your eyes. Last, watch your hands. Don't play with your hair or place your hands around your mouth. Being mindful of these little things will make you a better signer!

Good

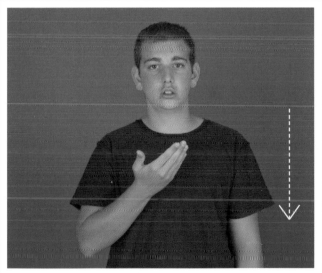

- *Good* uses both hands.

- The dominant hand will begin palm facing upward and horizontal at the bottom of your chin.

- The stationary hand will be horizontal, palm facing up.

- Move the dominant hand down until it rests in the stationary palm.

Week

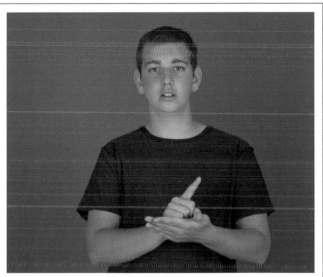

- *Week* uses both hands.

- The stationary palm will be face up, fingers together.

- The dominant hand will form the number *1* position.

- Slide the number *1* over the palm, beginning at the base and moving to the tips of the fingers.

WEEKEND ACTIVITIES
Encourage conversation beyond the water cooler—use e-mail and pictures to say more

Did you just come back from a trip? Have a nice holiday? See a good movie or read a good book? Or maybe your child scored the winning goal at the Saturday morning soccer game. All of your weekend activities are a great place to start a simple conversation with a deaf co-worker. In addition to the signs you are learning, help further the understanding

by bringing in pictures. Nothing shows what you are trying to communicate better than a picture of where you went or what your child did. Or, if you want to give more details about an event you saw, a trip you took, or something you want to discuss further, follow it up with an e-mail. You don't have to do all of your conversations with your hands. Those conver-

Movie

- *Movie* uses both hands.

- Each hand will form a number *5* position.

- Place the dominant palm on top of the passive palm.

- The hands will be facing palm to palm.

- Slide the dominant palm back and forth two times.

Skating

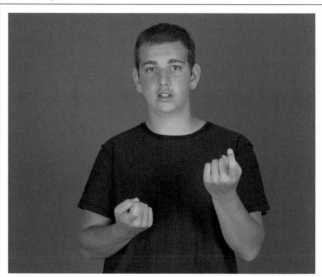

- *Skating* uses both hands.

- Form the letter *x* with both hands.

- Turn the *x* flat, making it sideways. Or, form the *x* upside down, as shown above.

- Alternately move each hand away from and back to the body again. The movement should mimic the motion of one skate moving in front of the other. It should look fluid like skating.

194

sation starters can help you begin an e-mail conversation.

In everyday conversation try to avoid the use of idioms such as "throw someone a bone" or "too many chiefs and not enough Indians" or "blow your own horn." The use of idioms is often difficult to explain and interpret. Instead, be direct with your comments without the use of idioms.

Here you will learn four signs that could involve normal weekend activities: *movie, skating, boating,* and *fishing.*

Boating

- *Boating* and *boat* are the same sign. Use both hands to form this sign.

- Cup the hands together to form a boat.

- The fingers will be closed together.

- Move the boat forward and slightly up and down as though it were moving over waves.

Fishing

- *Fishing* uses both hands.

- The passive hand will be gripped around an imaginary reel.

- The dominant hand will be gripped around an imaginary pole.

- Slightly move the arms simultaneously back and forth to mimic having a fish on the line.

TRAVEL TALK

Know how to talk on the TTY while using proper etiquette

Here are four signs to help discuss a trip or vacation. But, like many conversations you may run out of time before you are finished discussing your trip. If you want to extend your conversation consider using a TTY.

Although the Internet age is diminishing the use of TTYs (telephone teletype), many Deaf still communicate widely through the use of it. The TTY looks like a small typewriter with a digital screen. It relies on both parties having one, and both type messages back and forth, much like talking on an Internet instant messenger program. If one person doesn't have a TTY, he can use a relay service that interprets the call by relaying the typed messages back and forth. If you have a TTY or use a TTY in a public facility, try to follow some basic TTY etiquette:

1. Allow the phone to ring much longer than you normally would. Because the deaf person relies on seeing the flashing

How?

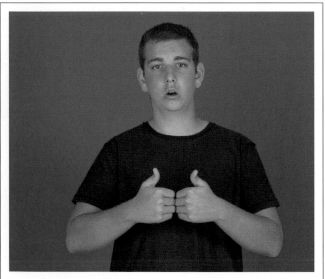

- *How* is a two-part sign. The first part will begin with both fists touching. The thumbs will be extended upward, while all other fingers are in a closed fist.

- The second part of the sign involves motion. Simultaneously move each fist away from each other.

- The final position of the sign will end with the thumbs pointing in the opposite direction from one another.

- Your face should be asking a question.

Travels or Trip

- *Travels, travel,* and *trip* are all the same sign and use the dominant hand.

- Form a broken letter *v* with your dominant hand. The index and middle fingers are the only fingers extended. All other fingers are closed.

- Move the hand in circular motions as you move the hand away from your body.

- The movement is representative of moving or going somewhere.

lights for the telephone it may take him a while to notice that the phone is ringing.

2. Begin conversation by stating who you are. For example, after you have made the call and the person has answered, identify yourself with your name and then GA like this: "This is Suzie GA."

3. Use GA when you finish saying what you have to say. GA stands for "go ahead." The person will not type a response until she has gotten this typed cue.

4. When you are ready to say goodbye, end conversation by saying "SKSK," which stands for stop keying.

5. Sometimes signals get jumbled, and the letters come through as odd letters or symbols. It is OK to ask "Can you read me?" to confirm that what you are typing came through correctly.

6. Some TTYs come with the ability to print out the conversation, which is helpful when a person gives an important date, address, or telephone number.

Nice

- *Nice* uses both hands.

- The dominant hand will be placed flat upon the stationary hand.

- The stationary hand will be palm facing upward, and

the dominant hand will be facing downward.

- In a sliding motion away from your body, slide the top hand across the bottom hand until it is completely off.

Pictures

- *Pictures* uses both hands.

- The passive palm will form a closed number *5* position, palm facing away from the body.

- The dominant hand will form the letter *c* position.

- Begin with the *c* placed beside your eye on the side of your face. Next, move the *c* downward until it rests squarely against the middle of the passive palm.

FAMILY CHITTER CHATTER

Communicating with the Deaf has never been easier through videophone or video relay services

The videophone is rapidly becoming the preferred method of communication for the Deaf. Videophones act much like web cameras, enabling the two deaf parties to see one another and communicate more easily. Yet, a videophone can be connected to a television so that the two parties have a much larger space in which to see one another. Videophones can also be connected to a laptop computer. The use of the videophone has allowed the Deaf community to speak in ASL with their deaf family and friends. Even if you don't have a videophone, you can still use this highly effective method of communication by using a video relay service. The deaf person and the video relay interpreter would see one an-

How?

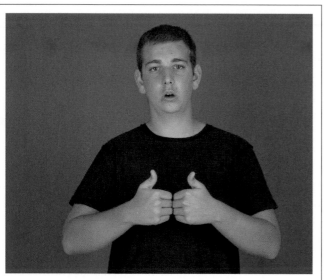

- *How* is a two-part sign. The first part will begin with both fists touching. The thumbs will be extended upward, while all other fingers are in a closed fist.

- The second part of the sign involves motion. Simultaneously move each fist away from each other.

- The final position of the sign will end with the thumbs pointing in opposite directions from one another.

- Your face should be asking a question.

Family

- *Family* uses both hands.

- Form the letter *f* for family with each hand. The index finger and thumb will touch, while the other three fingers are extended and spread apart.

- Begin with the tips of each *f* touching so that the index finger and thumb of each hand are touching and facing one another.

- Move the hands apart to form a half-circle until the hands meet again. Now the back sides of each hand are touching.

other through their videophones. The interpreter speaks to the hearing person through a telephone and communicates messages back and forth between the two parties.

When using a video relay service, be sure to observe good video relay etiquette:

Don't say "tell her" or "tell him." Instead, speak directly to the person on the other end of the conversation.

Don't speak too quickly and allow breaks between sentences to allow for translation. Don't change topics suddenly and speak about only one topic at a time.

Avoid speaking to the relay interpreter unless it is regarding a technical issue.

Wait until it is your turn to talk before you begin to say something. Be careful not to interrupt the other person.

Allow ample time for the phone call. Because the conversation is being translated, it will take longer than a hearing telephone call. If you need to stop before the conversation is over, be sure to let the other person know why.

Enjoy

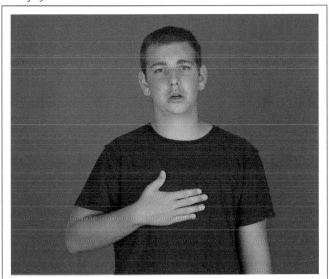

- *Enjoy* can be signed using one or two hands.

- Place the dominant or both hands on the chest, palm facing the chest.

- Move the palm around in a circle.

- Your face should reflect the sign.

Myself

- *Myself* uses the dominant hand only.

- Form a closed fist with the thumb extended upward.

- Place the fist in the middle of the chest.

- Move the hand on and off the chest very quickly one to two times. The hand will lift just off the chest before touching it again.

MORNING & AFTERNOON GREETINGS
Learn to greet your deaf neighbor friend, or coworker with these signs

It's easy to greet your fellow neighbor or friend using these signs. Just like you would with a hearing friend, it's important to take the time to greet your deaf friends, too. Remember that the deaf person wants to be talked to, to be included, and to be treated like a normal person.

Communicating with Care

• If a person has a cochlear implant or uses a hearing aid, be aware of her abilities or limitations. Don't assume you can talk to her with her back turned or from another room.

• Talking (or shouting) louder doesn't help. Just talk at a normal volume and speed.

• Remember that the deaf person wants to be talked to, to be included, and to be treated like a normal person.

Good

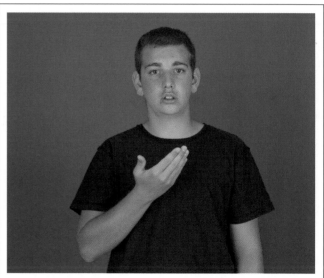

• *Good* uses both hands.

• The dominant hand will begin palm facing upward and horizontal at the bottom of your chin.

• The stationary hand will be horizontal, palm facing up.

• Move the dominant hand down until it rests in the stationary palm.

ZOOM

The cochlear implant is an electronic device made up of two parts. The external part is placed behind the ear. The internal part is surgically placed under the skin. The implant is made up of a microphone, a speech processor, a transmitter, and an electrode array. Those who are severely hard of hearing or deaf can benefit from the use of the implant. Contrary to popular belief, the implant does not restore hearing to normal levels. Rather, it helps the deaf or hard-of-hearing person through representative sounds and helps him understand what is being spoken. Because hearing from a cochlear implant is so different than normal hearing, it requires a great deal of therapy to be effective. Talk to your doctor for more information.

Afternoon

- *Afternoon* uses both the dominant hand and arm and the passive arm.

- The passive arm will be horizontally flat in front of your body. The palm is face down.

- Place the elbow of the dominant arm on the fingertips of the passive arm. Begin with the arm straight up and down.

- Next, move the arm downward until the palm rests on the passive arm.

Morning

- *Morning* uses both hands and arms.

- The passive arm will be horizontal in front of your body. The hand will rest inside the elbow of the dominant hand.

- The dominant arm will begin slightly broken and will move upward.

- The sign is symbolic of the sun rising in the morning.

NEWS & POLITICS

Enhanced education for the Deaf community allows for everyone to keep in touch with the latest world news

When it comes to being up to date on world news and politics, the Deaf community is as educated as everyone else. Institutions catered specifically for the Deaf allow for a greater education. Gallaudet University, located in Washington, D.C., promotes the intellectual, educational, and professional advancement of the Deaf and hard of hearing. Gallaudet University, the world's only university in which all programs and services are designed to accommodate deaf and hard-of-hearing students, was founded in 1864 by an act of Congress, and its charter was signed by President Abraham Lincoln. Students can choose from more than forty majors.

Even hearing students can attend Gallaudet, although those

Politics

- *Politics* uses the dominant hand only.

- Form the letter *p* for politics.

- Begin the sign with the *p* several inches away from the top of your head.

- Circle the *p* in the air beside the head one time. At the end of the circle motion, press the tip of the middle finger on the temple.

News

- *News* uses both hands.

- The passive hand is flat, palm up.

- The dominant hand will form the number *20* on top of the passive hand.

- Move the thumb and index finger together and apart while it is placed on the passive hand.

202

students cannot comprise more than 5 percent of each class. Gallaudet—or "Gally," as it is referred to by the students—allows many oral-based or mainstreamed students to meet other deaf and hard-of-hearing students who are just like they are. Unlike on other college campuses, these students find that they are like every other college kid. Rather than relying on interpreters, classes are signed by the professors in ASL. The facilities are tailored to best meet the needs of the Deaf. Gallaudet University has more than fifteen thousand alumni around the world.

ZOOM

Thomas Hopkins Gallaudet, father of deaf education in America, was inspired to teach through his deaf neighbor, Alice Cogswell. Through interaction, Gallaudet taught her to communicate. Hungry to learn more teaching methods, he studied under Laurent Clerc and Jean Massieu. Later, he established the American School for the Deaf. Gallaudet's son, Edward Miner Gallaudet, started Gallaudet University, named after his father.

Interesting

- *Interesting* uses the dominant hand only.

- Begin with the palm on top of the chest.

- Pull the hand away from the chest while closing the middle finger and thumb together.

Story

- *Story* uses both hands.

- Both hands will form the number *8*. One hand will start straight up and down, and the other hand will be sideways.

- Interlock both of the eights. Then pull them apart.

- Next, alternate which hand is straight and which hand is sideways. Interlock and pull apart again.

203

THE JEWISH FAITH

Programs and services to include the Jewish Deaf

Communicating with your fellow congregants is an essential element of faith. Learning ASL will enable you to learn from and teach the Deaf in your congregation. Here you will learn four signs to get you started: *temple, rabbi, Sabbath,* and *Jewish* or *Hebrew.* Being able to communicate will allow the deaf congregants to feel connected to fellow members. If services or classes are not communicated in ASL, deaf members will have greater challenges growing and learning in their faith.

Providing the faith in ASL, the deaf person's native tongue, allows the Deaf to learn more and better practice their faith. Instead of deaf congregants relying on speech reading, which they may or may not be able to do effectively, and the written translations of those nearby, they will be able to hear the services and classes in ASL, which will allow a better understanding and be more inclusive. If your congregation has deaf members, hire or find a volunteer interpreter to trans-

Temple

- *Temple* uses both hands.

- The passive hand can either be a closed fist or a flat palm.

- Form the letter *t* for temple with the dominant hand.

- Begin with the *t* several inches above the passive hand. Then place it on the hand. Repeat this motion.

Rabbi

- *Rabbi* uses both hands.

- Form the letter *r* for rabbi with each hand. The middle finger will cross the index finger.

- Place the hands just below each shoulder.

- Move the hands down the chest.

late the services. Consider programs that would encourage reaching out to young and old Deaf by offering classes and signed services. Helping deaf Jewish people connect with others who share their faith helps them to learn more about their faith and to feel a part of the community. The Deaf can be Included in the service, too, such as by having a deaf person stand next to the person reading and give the ASL translation. Encourage the Deaf to use ASL in responsive readings. Encourage deaf children to be included in the services and schooling at a very early age. Including the deaf participants will increase participation and add to the diversity within your temple.

The motion is symbolic of the sun setting, indicative of when the Sabbath begins.

Sabbath

- *Sabbath* uses both arms and hands. *Sabbath* is very similar to *afternoon.*

- Begin with the passive arm horizontal in front of your body, palm facing down.

- Form the letter *f* with the dominant hand. Place the dominant elbow on the fingertips of the passive hand.

- Begin with the *f* straight up and down. Move the *f* downward until it rests on the arm.

Jewish or Hebrew

- *Jewish* uses the dominant hand.

- Place the dominant hand on the chin. The thumb will be on one side of the chin. The remaining four fingers will be on the other side of the chin.

- Pull the hand downward, pulling the thumb to meet the fingers. The fingers are flat and closed together.

- This motion is symbolic of a gentleman's beard.

COMING OF AGE
Celebrate becoming a bar or bat mitzvah

When Jewish children reach the age of twelve (for a girl) or thirteen (for a boy), many choose to celebrate this coming of age. Girls, because of their tendency to mature earlier, celebrate this coming of age one year earlier. The coming of age means that the child is now accountable for her actions. No longer are the parents responsible if their child lies, steals, or otherwise causes trouble. Now the child is old enough to assume personal responsibility and observance of the Com-

mandments. Although a Jewish child automatically becomes a bar mitzvah or a bat mitzvah at age twelve or thirteen, the celebration that follows is not required. Yet, it is a wonderful time to celebrate the child's achievements. Following the service is often a reception. This celebration highlights the child's awareness of her faith and connection to Judaism. The young man or woman is encouraged to continue Jewish education beyond becoming a bar or bat mitzvah.

Bar Mitzvah: Part 1

- *Bar mitzvah* is a two-part sign using both hands and arms.

- Begin with saying the sign for *boy*.

- *Boy* is made by closing the dominant palm on the imaginary bill of a baseball cap.

- Your thumb will touch the four fingers as you close your palm together.

Bar Mitzvah: Part 2

- Extend the stationary arm horizontally in front of your body. The hand will be a closed fist.

- The dominant hand will form the letter *t*.

- Place the *t* on the arm so that the dominant arm is resting on the passive arm.

- Next, circle the arm and hand all the way around the stationary arm. After a full circle, place the arm and hand to rest on the arm again.

If you are inviting deaf friends or family to your child's celebration, consider how you can best include them. If possible, have an interpreter present for the ceremony. Print out ahead of time any pertinent information about the ceremony, what it means, and what to expect. If you have a seating arrangement, ensure that the deaf person is seated where the line of sight is not hindered.

If attending this special celebration, you'll no doubt want to honor the special girl or boy with a gift. If giving money, it is usually given in increments of eighteen, a number associated with good luck. Other suitable gifts are items appropriate for a birthday gift for a twelve- or thirteen-year-old.

Notice that the difference between these signs is saying boy or girl in front of mitzvah.

Bat Mitzvah: Part 1

- Form the sign *girl*. Make a closed fist with the thumb extended.

- Draw the thumb to the side of your chin.

- Brush your thumb downward two times.

Bat Mitzvah: Part 2

- Extend the stationary arm horizontally in front of your body. The hand will be a closed fist.

- The dominant hand will form the letter *t*.

- Place the *t* on the arm so that the dominant arm is resting on the passive arm.

- Next, circle the arm and hand all the way around the stationary arm. After a full circle, place the arm and hand to rest on the arm again.

CHURCH SIGNS
Reach out to the Deaf through worship and ministry

Perhaps you've decided to learn ASL in order to start or to be part of the deaf ministry in your church. It is mesmerizing to watch the beauty of songs being signed and to see the message translated into signs. Perhaps watching these signs has piqued your own interest, and now you want to become involved.

Learning ASL is the beginning of being able to be involved in a deaf ministry. ASL will give you the tools not only to in-

terpret but also to teach, learn from, and build a relationship with a new deaf person. If you are passionate about being involved in a deaf ministry, consider taking an ASL class. Through this book you will have sign language basics, but a class will give you the interaction you need to really develop your knowledge.

However, understanding the language is only the first step you need to work with the Deaf. You should also make every

Christian

- *Christian* uses the dominant hand.

- Form the letter *c* for Christ.

- Begin with the *c* placed at the shoulder opposite the hand you are signing with.

- Move the *c* diagonally across your chest to rest at the waist. It is now on the same side as the signing hand.

Church

- *Church* uses both hands.

- The passive arm will be placed horizontally in front of your body.

- Form the letter c for church with the dominant hand.

- Rest the *c* on top of the passive hand. Move the *c* up and down two times.

effort to understand Deaf culture and community. This is a process that will not happen in just a few days or weeks but rather through the regular investment of time. Growing the ministry will require that people learn about what you are doing. Consider alerting local Deaf clubs about your new ministry or new classes you are offering. Post information on your church website. If there is a deaf school or program, invite its participants and provide easy access to your programs. The Deaf are the greatest communicators for your program. If they come and like what they see and do, they will be eager to share the information with their deaf friends. Regularly visiting with and communicating with your deaf associates are effective ways to encourage them to visit your church. Have parties and other social events to encourage fellowship.

Preacher

- *Preacher* or *preach* uses the dominant hand only.

- Form the letter *g* with the dominant hand. Place the *g* at the base of the throat, resembliing the collar of a priest.

- Another version of preacher uses the letter *f*. Place the hand near your temple. Use the same side of your head as the hand that you are signing with.

- Move the *f* forward and back several times.

Song and Sing

- *Song* and *sing* are the same sign and use both arms.

- The passive arm will be placed horizontally flat in front of your body.

- Form the letter *b* with the dominant hand. Move the hand back and forth over the passive arm.

- The dominant hand will not touch the passive arm.

THE TRINITY
Sign and sing praise and worship through ASL

Praise and worship are important elements of any church service. Worship is a time to leave the distractions of everything else behind and focus on the message. Praise and worship are equally important in a Deaf ministry. Although the music may not be heard, the Deaf worship through song. If you are interested in singing in ASL, think about the following tips:

What is the song trying to say? Think about the overall mes-

sage of the song. The words do not have to be translated word for word.

Don't worry about the beat of the music. You are conveying the overall message, and the signs you are signing do not have to fall into the same place as the words would.

Overemphasize your signs. Generally, in song, the signs are larger and more dramatic. Flow one sign into the next without breaking your hands at your side.

God

- *God* uses the dominant hand.

- Form the letter *b* with your hand.

- Begin the motion with the *b* in front of your face.

- Move the *b* upward above your head. Then bring it downward just in front of the forehead.

Jesus

- *Jesus* is formed using both hands.

- The motion will alternate with each hand. You may begin with either hand.

- Place the middle finger of one hand in the middle

of the opposite hand. The other fingers will remain stretched.

- Next, switch hands and repeat the motion.

Don't be afraid to use your face and body. Your face is communicating the song. Feel the words and show the meaning of the words.

Act out or demonstrate the song as much as you can. For example, if the song talks about a person praying, look as though you were praying. Or if the person is talking to God, then posture your body and face as though you were talking to God.

Here you will learn the signs *God*, *Jesus*, and *Holy Trinity*. These three signs are common words in many praise and worship songs.

Trinity: Part 1

- *Trinity* uses both hands.

- Begin by forming the number *3* with the dominant hand. The thumb and index and middle fingers will be extended. All other fingers will be closed.

- Face the palm toward your body.

Trinity: Part 2

- After saying *3* representing God, Jesus, and the Holy Spirit, you want to demonstrate how they represent one thing.

- Next, cover the *3* with the passive hand. Pull the *3* through the passive hand.

- The dominant hand will now form the number *1*. The sign will end with the number *1* sign.

SIGNS IN SERVICE
Deaf churches designed specifically to meet the needs of the Deaf community

Deaf churches are operated by deaf individuals specifically to meet the needs of the Deaf and hard-of-hearing community. Although there are some independent deaf churches, most deaf churches are branches or ministries of larger churches. Usually those on staff are deaf; the worship leaders are deaf, as are the elders or deacons in the church. The service and worship are performed in ASL and usually accompanied by spoken English for the hard of hearing or KODAs.

Many Deaf choose to go to a deaf church because it provides them a place to worship and to have community with people who are just like they are. Instead of depending on a person to interpret the service, they are directly a part of the service, and

Bless

- *Bless* uses both hands.

- Begin with both hands in a flat *o* shape. The fingertips will face the forehead.

- Next, move the hands away from the forehead and turn

the hands to face away from your body.

- Open your hands to open palms as though you were releasing or giving the blessing.

Baptize

- *Baptize* uses both hands.

- Both hands will be in a thumbs-up position. Hold the hands in front of your chest.

- Move the thumbs simultaneously and in the same direction side to side.

- The action of the sign represents someone being immersed in baptism.

the message is aimed squarely at the deaf audience. Much like hearing church groups, these bodies function much like a family and are a regular source of socialization as well.

Many areas simply don't have a deaf population large enough to support a deaf church. In smaller regions or regions where there is a small deaf population, a deaf ministry in which the service is interpreted is used instead. In deaf ministries it is helpful for there to be a section designated for the deaf to sit together, close to the front where they can see the message clearly.

Holy

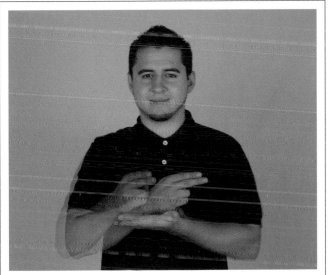

- *Holy* has many variations, depending on the region and church body you are in. Ask your deaf members which variation they prefer.

- This widely used variation of *holy* uses both hands.

- The passive hand is face up and flat.

- Form the letter *h* with the dominant hand. Sweep the *h* across the passive hand. The *h* will not touch the hand but will hover just above it.

Love

- *Love* uses both arms.

- Cross one arm over the other arm, forming a large x shape on your chest.

- The fists are closed and tight.

- Be careful of hand placement. If the hands are open and not closed, you will be saying *rest*.

213

THE MESSAGE
The use of iconic signs makes signing simpler

Iconic signs, as you may have already noticed, are a large part of ASL. Iconic signs, or signs whose shape, formation, or movement closely represents the actual image of the word, tend to be easier to remember and use than other signs. In religious signs many are iconic. Some of those signs include:

Altar: This sign is made by bringing both thumbs together with the fists closed. Draw the thumbs apart as though you were pulling them along the top of a table. Then draw the thumbs down as though they were the legs of a table or altar.

Heart: Using both index fingers, simply draw a heart on your chest near your heart.

Crown: Both hands will look as though they were placing a crown on the top of the head. The palms should be facing downward.

Hidden: This sign is similar to *hide*. Form the letter *a* with your dominant hand, beginning with the thumb touching

Sin

- *Sin* has many versions in ASL. Again, refer to your deaf members to see which version is preferred.

- This widely used version of *sin* uses both hands.

- Form the number *1* with both hands.

- Hold each number *1* directly in front of you. Make two large circles with your arms. End the sign with both number *1s* front of your chest.

Cross

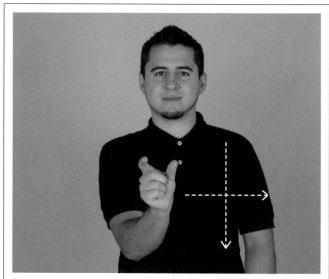

- *Cross* uses the dominant hand.

- Form the letter *c*. Or, use the index finger and thumb to form a *c*-like shape, as shown above

- Begin by drawing the first part of the cross in the air with the *c*.

- Next, draw the second side-to-side shape of a cross with the letter *c*.

the lips. Then "hide" the *a* underneath the downward-facing hand.

Offer/offering/present: All of these words can be said using one sign. Bring both hands, palms facing upward, one slightly in front of the other. Move them in an upward fashion as though you were offering something up or presenting something.

Pope: The hands will be representing the shape of the miter worn by the pope. Move both hands on either side of the head, making a double arc similar to the miter.

Power or *strength:* Grip together the fists of both hands, indicating strength or power. The hands will be in closed *s* fists moving outward from the body with force.

Scripture or *writings:* The dominant hand "writes" on the flat, open-faced passive hand.

Here you will learn four commonly used signs in a sermon or message: *sin, cross, death,* and *resurrection.*

Death

- *Death* uses both hands.

- Begin with one palm face up and one palm face down.

- Simultaneously turn the palms over so that the one that began as face up is now face down. The one that began as face down is now face up.

Resurrection

- *Resurrection* uses both hands.

- The passive hand will be flat, palm facing downward.

- The dominant hand will form the letter *u.* Place the tips of the *u* on the passive palm.

- Move the *u* upward, forming the shape of the written *m* in the air.

215

STUDYING THE BIBLE
Signing provides everyone with the opportunity to learn

Some churches struggle with the issue of whether to compensate those who interpret the services. The interpreters are providing a much-needed service for the deaf members. Interpreting takes a great deal of time, skill, and education. While translating the person not only must translate but also hear what is being spoken and constantly be actively listening while signing. It can be physically exhausting to keep up, and that is why for events lasting longer than an hour most

interpreters team translate, signing in about twenty-minute periods. Most interpreters are self-employed and must pay to be recertified annually. Last, the service that the interpreters provide enables the deaf members to be a part of the service, to be connected to the group, to learn from the service. So, should these important people be volunteers?

If your church or synagogue has a certified interpreter who willingly wants to give her services as a form of contribution

Bible

Many religious signs have many versions. When in doubt which one you should use, ask!

- *Bible* is made by first making the sign for *Jesus,* followed by the sign for *book*.

- Place the middle finger of one hand in the middle of the opposite hand. The other fingers will remain stretched.

- Next, switch hands and repeat the motion.

- Last, make the sign for *book* by pressing both palms together and then opening the palms flat to resemble an open book.

Study

- *Study* uses both hands.

- The passive hand will represent the book or paper you are studying.

- Next, wiggle the fingers of the dominant hand over the passive hand.

to the church, then this contribution is similar to a donation that any other professional might offer to the church. In such cases it is entirely appropriate to recognize and thank this person with a gift certificate or other type of tangible thanks. If no certified interpreters volunteer to provide their services for free, a church body should not hesitate to hire one. These individuals are professionals and generate their living from interpreting. To expect individuals to interpret without compensation is to ignore the valuable service they are providing to the church body. Further, it communicates that interpret-

ing for the Deaf is not important enough for church funds. Through quality interpretive services you are communicating not only the sermon but also a sense of value and welcome to the Deaf community.

Glory

- *Glory* uses both hands.

- The passive hand is flat and open.

- Place the middle finger of the dominant hand in the center of the passive palm.

- Pull the finger away from the palm moving upward. Move the hand slightly back and forth as you pull the hand up.

Amen

- *Amen* uses both hands.

- Press both hands together, fingers closed in a praying position.

- You can nod your head downward as you press the palms together.

- Your expression should be serious.

SIGNING THE WORD
Easy steps to creating a deaf-friendly wedding or funeral

If you are planning a wedding or a funeral and expect to have a sizable deaf crowd in attendance, be considerate of the deaf needs. These tips should help make the event better for your deaf attendees:

Don't skimp on the interpreter. Hire a certified interpreter. Consider the importance of what is being communicated. If it is remembering the life of a loved one or witnessing two lives being joined together, this is not a time for broken sign language. Placement of the interpreter is essential. Have the interpreter near where the action happens so that the deaf persons won't miss out on seeing the action. If possible, elevate the interpreter to ensure all attendees can clearly see the hand movements.

Group all Deaf near the interpreter. Keep flowers, candles, and other arrangements out of the line of vision. Ensure that centerpieces don't overpower the communication space. At

Angel

- *Angel* uses both hands.

- Begin with the tips of the fingers of each hand placed on either shoulder.

- Next, move the hands outward, as pictured above.

- Move the hands slightly up and down, illustrating how an angel's wings might flutter.

Lord

- *Lord* uses the dominant hand.

- Form the letter *l* for *Lord*. Place the *l* on the opposite shoulder of the signing hand.

- Move the *l* diagonally across the chest to rest on the waist of the same side as the signing hand.

the reception afterward it is appropriate to continue to have an interpreter to translate important toasts or remembrances.

Don't dim the lights too much. Although you might be looking for a romantic setting, the dim lights make it difficult to see and read signs. Turn the lights up enough that signing can easily be read.

Instead of clinking a glass, wave a napkin to grab attention and make a toast. Turn the music up. The Deaf, too, enjoy dancing. Loud music will help the Deaf hear music through vibrations.

Being aware of your audience will help the wedding or funeral be something everyone can be a part of.

Here are two common Christian phrases to add to your signing vocabulary: *angel of the Lord* and *attributes or characteristics of God*. The more phrases and signs you can learn, the less you will rely on finger spelling or using gestures for words and the more understanding you will have!

Attributes or Characteristics of God: Part 1

- *Attributes* or *characteristics* is made with both hands.

- Begin with both hands forming the letter *f*. Interlock the two.

- Draw the hands apart with the dominant hand higher than the passive hand.

- *Characteristics* can also be signed by circling the letter *c* around a vertical flat palm. The *c* then ends against the vertical palm of the passive hand.

Attributes or Characteristics of God: Part 2

- After saying *characteristics of* or *attributes* of, finish the phrase by adding *God*.

- Form the letter *b* with your hand.

- Begin the motion with the *b* in front of your face.

- Move the *b* upward above your head. Then bring it downward just in front of the forehead.

OLD & NEW TESTAMENT

Deaf missions are reaching the Deaf across the globe for Christ

What is a deaf mission? A mission is a group of people whose members travel to a foreign country to share their faith with the individuals of that country. Deaf missions are different from normal missions because they attempt to reach those who are deaf and hard of hearing in foreign countries. Of the millions of Deaf around the world, very few have been exposed to religious training. Historically, because of the communication barrier, many Deaf have been left out of religious practices. In many emerging countries the communication barrier still exists and hinders the efforts of other missions whose members cannot communicate with the deaf or hard of hearing.

Because sign language is the native tongue for most Deaf worldwide, deaf missions primarily attempt to reach these unreached people through the use of sign language rather than printed text, which they may or may not be able to

Old

- *Old* uses only one hand.

- Form the letter *o* with the dominant hand; all fingers will be closed together, fingertips resting on the thumb.

- Place the thumb side of the *o* on the bottom of your chin.

- Pull the *o* away from your chin. The older the person is, the longer you will draw the *o* down.

New

- *New* uses both hands.

- The passive hand will be palm up, flat, and still.

- The dominant hand will also be palm up. Slightly curve the palm and brush it against the passive palm several times.

understand. Because of the cultural barriers between the Deaf and the hearing, it is fitting that the Deaf reach other Deaf and establish churches and services for these people. Reaching and teaching these people go beyond just providing an interpreter. Through curriculum written for the Deaf and visual modes of teaching the Deaf are taught in their first language. Beyond teaching the Gospel, many deaf missions attempt to improve the quality of life by teaching sign language courses and establishing schools, job training, medical services, and more.

Testament: Part 1

- *Testament* uses both hands.

- Form the letter *t* with the dominant hand.

- The passive hand is vertical, flat, and still.

- Move the *t* from the top of the hand to the base of the hand.

Testament: Part 2

Testament is like many religious signs that have many variations.

- Another common way to sign testament uses both hands forming the *8* shape.

- Make the same motion as you would to form the word *story* on page 203 but emphasize the range of the sign. The hands will begin as interlocked *8s* but will come apart farther.

SCRIPTURE SIGNS

Encourage deaf awareness in your church or place of worship

Deaf Awareness Week occurs the last full week of September, although your congregation can choose to have a deaf awareness week anytime of the year. Setting aside an awareness week is a great way to let the community, church, or temple learn more about your ministry and about the Deaf. To encourage awareness, consider conducting some of the following events at your church or temple:

Offer free hearing screenings: Over time people's hearing diminishes. It is estimated that one in ten people could benefit from the use of a hearing aid but either does not realize that she has a problem or doesn't seek hearing screenings. Regular hearing screenings should be a part of everybody's health regimen.

Offer free ASL classes: Provide courses for people in the community to learn ASL. Education: Provide information on the causes and effects of hearing loss.

Book of

- Use these two signs to form the phrase *Book of Life*. *Book* uses both hands.

- Begin with the palms pressed together.

- Open the palms to lie flat, resembling an open book.

Life

- *Life* uses both hands.

- Both hands will be in a thumbs-up position.

- Begin with both hands about waist level.

- Move both hands up simultaneously until the hands are at about chest level.

Have a "silent" meal or function: Share a meal or an activity during which the only words that are spoken are signed.

Have a videophone relay demonstration: Set up a booth demonstrating how to use a video relay service. Educate the audience on how to make a call and equip members with relay service phone numbers.

Through deaf awareness activities, perhaps your congregation members will grow in their knowledge of the Deaf. Attempting to inform the members of the congregation about the Deaf culture and tools they can use to communicate with the Deaf will help diminish the communication barriers within your congregation. Ultimately your congregation members may walk away with the realization that the Deaf are not so different, that aside from hearing they, too, are regular people!

Eternal

- *Eternal* uses both hands.

- Each hand will have a closed fist with the thumb extended.

- Touch the tips of the two thumbs together.

- Move the hands simultaneously forward. Another version of this sign is to make the same motion but in the letter *y* position.

Mercy

Alternate versions of *mercy* have both palms and middle finger directed toward the person being addressed.

- *Mercy* uses both hands.

- Both hands will have the middle finger bent forward. The rest of the fingers will be spread apart.

- The dominant hand will be slightly higher than the passive hand.

- Move each hand in circles in alternating directions.

REPENTING & FORGIVING
Encourage Deaf participation in your church or temple body

Encouraging participation in the work of the church can often be a daunting task. Nursery or preschool workers are often in short supply, the office could always use a little more help, and information desk and website needs are often in short supply. Encourage the Deaf congregants to get involved. Although they may not be able to pick up the phone and answer a call in the office, there are still many ways they can actively participate and help your church or temple body:

Operating the information desk: What better way to meet and greet new deaf people as they come through the door? Having a deaf person accessible to greet a new deaf or hard-of-hearing visitor shows that the Deaf are important to your body.

Newsletter or bulletin information: Regularly have your deaf ministry print an article about what is happening in your ministry. If you are having a social event or meeting, in-

Forgive

- *Forgive* and *excuse* are the same sign.

- *Forgive* will use both hands.

- The passive hand is flat, palm up, and still.

- The dominant hand will brush across the hand as though it were sweeping something away.

Repent

- *Repent* and *sorry* are the same sign.

- Place the dominant hand on the chest. The hand is in the letter *a* position.

- Make several small circles on the chest with the hand.

form the community. Encourage the Deaf to help with other newsletter needs, too!

Infant or preschool workers: One of the best advantages to being deaf is that you can't hear a screaming baby. Hearing is not required to work with babies or toddlers. Rocking, feeding, and loving on the little ones can all be accomplished without hearing.

Writing curriculum for small groups: Because many Deaf learn through ASL, consider having Bible studies and small group curriculum written by a Deaf member who can spe-cifically develop a visually based curriculum.

Hospitality helpers: Need help setting out the coffee and donuts or greeting people as they come through the door? You don't need to hear to help.

Teachers for ASL classes: Encourage the hard of hearing or Deaf to teach or help facilitate an ASL class.

Here you will learn the signs: *forgive, repent,* and *free will.* These common Christian phrases can be used in service, worship, Bible study, and more.

Free

- *Free* uses both hands and arms.

- Begin in the *love* position with both arms crossed, fists closed.

- Next, break apart the arms until each arm is directly in front of your body.

Will

- *Will* uses the dominant hand.

- Begin by placing the dominant hand on the chest. The hand will be flat, fingers together and thumb extended.

- Move the hand outward away from the body.

225

SIGNING THE SERVICE
Equip yourself to talk in a new tongue

Now that you've made it through nineteen chapters of ASL, you are equipped to begin communicating in a new language. Equipped now with the alphabet and numerous phrases and words and with a knowledge of the Deaf culture, you are ready to begin participating in the Deaf world. Use the resource guide in Chapter 20 to get more ideas of how better to become immersed in the Deaf world. Opportunity exists all around you. Look into local deaf schools or

programs, churches, deaf theater groups, clubs, and more in your community. Sign up for an ASL class at your local community college or church. Take the time and make the effort to use the skills you have learned.

Practicing your new language is the way you will become proficient. Spending time with deaf people will teach you how to better use your body and facial expressions. Observing the Deaf as they speak will help increase your awareness

Son

- These next two signs can be used to form the phrase *Son of God* by combining *Son* and *God*.

- *Son* uses both arms.

- The passive arm will be horizontally extended in front of you.

- The dominant hand will begin at the top of the forehead. Move the hand downward until it rests on the passive arm.

Of God

- After saying *Son*, next form *God*. The *of* does not need to be said in ASL.

- Form the letter *b* with your hand.

- Begin the motion with the *b* in front of your face.

- Move the *b* upward above your head. Then bring it downward just in front of the forehead.

of the importance of emotion and emphasis with your signs. The more you use your new language, the less you will rely on writing on pen and paper or using gestures to communicate. It is always a good idea to have an ASL dictionary handy to look up words that you may not know.

Don't give up or get discouraged. As with any new language, fluency takes time and practice. If your first attempts at communication fail, keep a good attitude. The person you are speaking to will have patience and will want to help you communicate. Ask if the person understands you and be sure to speak up if you can't understand him. Communication is a two-way street, so make sure you both are on the same page. Last, relax. You have the knowledge. Just enjoy putting your new communication skills to work.

Here you will find the three final signs used in Christian services and educational classes: *Son, of God,* and *heaven.*

Heaven: Part 1

- *Heaven* uses both hands.

- Begin with each palm facing downward.

- The dominant hand will begin above the passive hand.

- Rotate the hands around one another several times.

Heaven: Part 2

- The second part of heaven is made by drawing the two hands apart.

- The sign will end, as pictured, with both bent palms horizontal to the ground. The palms are facing downward.

- Some people choose to gaze upward as they form the sign, as though they were looking toward heaven.

DEAF COMMUNITY ORGANIZATIONS

Congratulations on your new signing skills! Please dive into these additional resources to help strengthen and develop your knowledge of ASL. Though this listing is by far not a comprehensive list of all of the available resources, it is a good place to start.

The Americans with Disabilities Act (ADA)

The ADA is the federal law protecting all Americans with disabilities. As it pertains to the Deaf, this law gives specific protections for accommodations and communication for workplaces, medical providers, and more.
www.ada.gov

For issues related to employment or work accommodation:
www.eeoc.gov

For issues related to transportation accommodation:
www.fta.dot.gov/civilrights/civil_rights_2360

For issues related to telephone accommodation or relay services:
www.fcc.gov/cgb/dro/trs

For issues related to educational services:
www.ed.gov/about/offices/list/ocr/index

For issues related to medical service providers:
www.hhs.gov/ocr/index

C.O.D.A. International

A nonprofit international organization servicing both CODAs (adult children of deaf adults) and KODAs (kids of deaf adults) and aimed at connecting hearing adults and KODAs who share a bicultural and bilingual experience.
www.coda-international.org

Deaf Clubs

For a comprehensive listing of Deaf clubs across the country, visit www.deafconnect.com/deaf/clubs

Deaf Sports Organizations

American Hearing Impaired Hockey Association
www.ahiha.org

Deaf International Basketball Federation
www.dibf.org

International Committee of Sports for the Deaf
www.deaflympics.com

Texas Deaf Sports Association
texasdeafsports.wordpress.com

United States Deaf Cycling Association
www.usdeafcycling.org

USA Deaf Soccer
www.usdeafsoccer.com

USA Deaf Sports Federation
www.usdeafsports.org

Deaf Cultural Arts

Arizona Deaf Theatre
www.arizonadeaftheatre.com

Deaf West Theatre
www.deafwest.org

Gallaudet Dance Company
dance.gallaudet.edu

InterAct Children's Theatre for the Deaf
www.discoveret.org/interact

National Theatre of the Deaf
www.ntd.org

Families with a Deaf or Hard of Hearing Child

American Society for Deaf Children
www.deafchildren.org

BEGINNINGS for Parents of Children Who Are Deaf or Hard of Hearing
www.ncbegin.org

The Children's Treehouse
www.deaffun.homestead.com

John Tracy Clinic
www.jtc.org

Junior National Association of the Deaf
www.nad.org/jrnad

Laurent Clerc National Deaf Education Center Public Relations Products and Training
clerccenter.gallaudet.edu

National Association of Parents with Children in Special Education
www.napcse.org

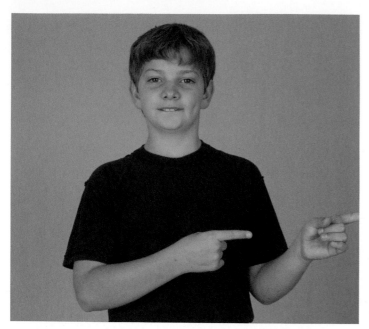

National Dissemination Center for Children with Disabilities (NICHCY)
www.nichcy.org

National Information Clearinghouse on Children Who are Deaf-Blind
www.dblink.org

U.S. Department of Health and Human Services, *Stop Bullying Now,
Bullying Among Children and Youth*
www.stopbullyingnow.hrsa.gov

First Aid & Safety Resources

Emergency preparedness: what to do in an emergency:
American College of Emergency Physicians www.3acep.org

"Steps to take to get the most out of a doctor visit":
www.wrongdiagnosis.com/diagnosis/steps-doctors-visit

"How Do I Know When 'It's Time for Hospice'?" Compassionate Care
Alliance Caring Resources Guide
www.caringresources.org/hospice/how_do_i_know

Emergency Preparedness for Your Special Needs Child Resource
Guide
www.cshcn.org/resources/emergencypreparedness

Gallaudet University

Gallaudet is the only liberal arts university in the world designe
specifically to accommodate the unique peer and communicatio
needs of deaf and hard-of-hearing students. Gallaudet is located i
Washington, D.C.

800 Florida Avenue, NE
Washington, DC 20002
www.Gallaudet.edu

Interpreter Services, Organizations,
& Information

Conference of Interpreter Trainers
www.cit-asl.org

Laurent Clerc, National Deaf Education Center, Gallaudet University
"Becoming a Sign Language Interpreter"
clerccenter.gallaudet.edu/InfoToGo/357

National Alliance of Black Interpreters
www.naobi.org

Registry of Interpreters for the Deaf
www.rid.org

National Deaf Organizations

ADARA: Professionals Networking for Excellence in Service Deliver
with Individuals Who Are Deaf or Hard of Hearing
www.adara.org

American Association of the Deaf-Blind
www.aadb.org

Association of Late-Deafened Adults
www.alda.org

American Society for Deaf Children
www.deafchildren.org

The Ear Foundation
www.earfoundation.org

Episcopal Conference of the Deaf
www.ecdeaf.com

The George Washington University Health Resource Center
www.health.gwu.edu
Hear Now
www.sotheworldmayhear.org

Helen Keller National Center for Deaf-Blind Youths and Adults
www.HKNC.org

Intertribal Deaf Council, Inc.
www.deafnative.com

Jewish Deaf Congress
www.jewishdeafcongress.org

League for the Hard of Hearing
www.lhh.org

National Asian Deaf Congress
www.nadc-usa.org

National Association of the Deaf
NAD is a nonprofit organization that seeks to empower and protect the deaf and hard of hearing through advocacy of issues relating to the Deaf.
www.nad.org

National Black Deaf Advocates
www.nbda.org

National Captioning Institute
www.ncicap.org

National Catholic Office of the Deaf
www.ncod.org

National Consortium on Deaf-Blindness
www.nationaldb.org

National Council of Hispano Deaf and Hard of Hearing
www.nchdhh.org

National Fraternal Society of the Deaf
www.NFSD.com

National Institute on Deafness and Other Communication Disorders
Information Clearinghouse
www.nidcd.nih.gov

National Technical Institute for the Deaf
www.rit.edu/NTID

Speech & Language Pathology/ Audiology

American Speech-Language-Hearing Association
www.asha.org

House Ear Institute
www.hei.org

International Hearing Society
www.ihsinfo.org

Vestibular Disorders Association
www.vestibular.org

Telephone & Videophone Relay Services

AT&T Relay Services
All Users: 711
TTY Users: (800) 855-2880
Voice Users: (800) 855-2881
PC Users: (800) 855-2882
Over the Internet:
www.relaycall.com/national/relay

Sprint Relay Services
Voice users for video relay service: (866) 410-5787
For a full description of all Sprint relay services, see www.sprint
relay.com

Sorenson Video Relay Service
(866) FAST-VRS (1 866 327-8877)

Telecommunications for the Deaf and Hard of Hearing, Inc. (TDI, Inc.)
A consumer advocacy group dedicated to equal access in tele-communications for the deaf and hard of hearing.
www.tdi-online.org

Web sites for & about the Deaf Community

All Deaf
www.alldeaf.com

Deaf.com
www.deaf.com

About.com
deafness.about.com

ONLINE GAMES & DICTIONARIES
Ready to test your skills? Visit these Web sites for fun games and puzzles

Now that you have a pretty good grasp on some sign language skills, put your knowledge to the test. The following websites offer a variety of puzzles and games that will challenge your memory. Have fun!

www.apples4theteacher.com/asl
Want to quiz yourself on the go? Here you can print off American Manual alphabet flashcards to use in the car, at home, or anywhere you have a quick minute.

www.aslpro.com/games
Visit this Web site to play hangman, What am I?, Find a Match, and

ASL Jeopardy. You'll also find a great signing online dictionary if yo want to learn additional signs.

asl.ms/
Think you're pretty good at reading the American Manual Alphabet? A this Web site pick the speed you are comfortable with. A random wor will be finger spelled in the box. Type the word the fingers are spellin and see if you are correct. Increase the speed for more challenge!

www.lifeprint.com/asl101
This is an excellent Web site for both ASL teachers and students. No

only will you find free ASL lessons, but many fun games to practice with including: practice quizzes, spelling quizzes, animated spelling quizzes, practice sheets, ASL word search, and more.

commtechlab.msu.edu/sites/aslweb/browser
Want to learn more signs? This ASL browser provides a large index of signs to click and see the word being signed. Add more words to your vocabulary here.

www.handspeak.com
This comprehensive Web site has a wealth of information from an online dictionary, ASL grammar, the American Manual Alphabet, International Sign Language, ASL Storytelling and more. Visit this Web site to increase your knowledge of ASL and learn more signs.

www.needsoutreach.org/Pages/sl
If you are a teacher this is a site for you. Learn specific signs for subjects such as biology, geography, elementary and secondary math, history, and more.

www.deafblind.com/worldsig
Here you will find links to international sign language dictionaries including German, Greek, Russian, Spanish, and more.

235

FINGERPLAY LYRICS
Song lyrics to sing with your toddler

For more song ideas visit
www.kididdles.com

"The Itsy Bitsy Spider"
Itsy, bitsy, spider went up the water spout
(Climb up arm.)
Down came the rain
(Wiggle fingers down from head to waist.)
And washed the spider out
(Throw arms to sides.)
Out came the sun and dried up all the rain
(Raise hands above head, make circle for sun.)
Now the itsy, bitsy spider
Went up the spout again.
(Climb up arm again.)

"Twinkle, Twinkle Little Star"
Written by Jane Taylor
Twinkle, twinkle, little star,
   (Wiggle fingers above head.)
How I wonder what you are.
   (Place index finger on forehead.)
Up above the world so high,
   (Point to the sky.)
Like a diamond in the sky.
   (Flash fingers out and in.)
Twinkle, twinkle, little star,
   (Wiggle fingers above head.)
How I wonder what you are!
 (Place index finger on forehead.)

"Baby Bumblebee"
I'm bringing home a baby bumblebee,
Won't my mommy be so proud of me,
(Cup both hands together as if holding bee.)
I'm bringing home a baby bumblebee,

Ouch! It stung me!
(Shake hands as if just stung.)

I'm squishing up the baby bumblebee,
Won't my mommy be so proud of me,
(Smash the bee between palms of hands.)
I'm squishing up a baby bumblebee,
Ooh! It's yucky!
(Open up hands to look at the smashed mess.)

I'm wiping off the baby bumblebee,
Won't my mommy be so proud of me,
(Wipe both hands off on clothes.)
I'm wiping off the baby bumblebee,
Now my mommy won't be mad at me!
(Hold hands up to show they are clean.)

RESOURCES

236

"Where Is Thumbkin"

Where is thumbkin? Where is thumbkin?
(Both hands are behind the back)
Here I am! Here I am!
(Bring left thumb to the front, follow with right thumb)
How are you today, sir?
(Wiggle left thumb back and forth as though it is talking)
Very well I thank you.
(Wiggle right thumb back in response)
Run away, run away
(Hide left hand behind back, follow with right hand behind back)
(Continue same motions with corresponding fingers)
Where is pointer?
Where is tall man?
Where is ring man?
Where is pinky?
(End song with all five fingers representing the family)
Where is family? Where is family?
(hide both hands behind back)
Here we are! Here we are!
(Show left hand all fingers spread apart, followed by right hand all fingers spread apart)
How are you today, sirs?
(Wiggle fingers of left hand)
Very well, we thank you!
(Wiggle fingers of right hand in response)
Run away, run away
(Hide left hand behind back, follow with right hand behind back)

GLOSSARY OF TERMS

American Manual Alphabet: The twenty-six handshapes that comprise the signed equivalent of the English alphabet. These letters are used to spell words.

Americans with Disabilities Act (ADA): The federal law protecting all Americans with disabilities. As it pertains to the Deaf, this law gives specific protections for accommodations and communication for workplaces, medical providers, and more.

cochlear implant: A surgically implanted electronic device that stimulates nerve endings in the inner ear in order to receive and process sounds.

CODA: Stands for "child of a deaf adult." These individuals are adults who were raised as children of deaf adults.

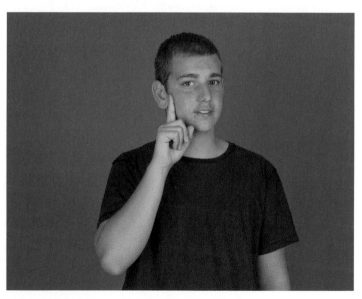

Contact Sign Language: One of several types of sign language i use in the United States. It is characterized by using signs in Englis word order and borrows elements from ASL and English.

deaf: "Deaf" with a lowercase "d" refers to those persons who sustai hearing loss and have lost the ability to hear for the purposes of ev eryday communication.

Deaf: Deaf with a capital "D" refers to people who associate the identity with the Deaf culture and whose primary language is Amer can Sign Language (ASL).

Deaf culture: The common and shared experiences of a collectiv group of Deaf individuals who use ASL as their primary language The Deaf culture experience is marked by shared social interaction beliefs, feelings, organizations, and often educational experiences.

finger spelling: Spelling words with handshapes of the America Manual Alphabet.

GA (go ahead): The term used in TTY or TDD conversations to ind cate to the person that he or she may "go ahead" and talk.

Gallaudet University: The only liberal arts university in the worl designed specifically to accommodate the unique peer and com munication needs of deaf and hard-of-hearing students. Gallaudet located in Washington, D.C.

gesture: The attempt to use the body, hands, face, or body motio to convey an idea or message.

handshape: How the fingers and palm are formed when making sign.

hard of hearing: Describes individuals who have some residual hearing but have experienced some hearing loss. Often these individuals gain hearing with the use of a hearing aid.

hearing aid: An electronic device that amplifies all sounds to the ear.

iconic signs: Signs that resemble closely the object they represent.

interpreter: A person who translates spoken English into ASL or ASL into spoken English.

KODA: Stands for "kid of a deaf adult." This term is used to refer to children who are being raised by deaf adults and are characterized by being bicultural, part of both the hearing and Deaf cultures.

mainstreaming: An educational term for the integration of deaf children (or other children with disabilities) into hearing public classrooms.

oralism: An educational method of teaching the deaf without the use of sign language through the primary use of speech reading.

sign language: A global method of communication in which deaf people exchange ideas and concepts through the use of their hands, expressions, and body language.

Signed Exact English: SEE is a form of sign language spoken in the United States. SEE is characterized by a one to one correspondence of English words to signed words emphasizing English syntax and grammar.

SK (Stop Keying): The abbreviation for "stop keying" used in TTY or TDD conversations to indicate that the conversation is ending.

speech reading: The ability to read what a person is saying by observing lip, mouth, and tongue movements.

TTY: Teletypewriter, also known as a TDD, which translates messages through a telephone line. The TTY has a screen on which to read messages and a keyboard to send messages.

INDEX

INDEX